METAL ON ICE

METAL ON ICE

TALES FROM CANADA'S HARD ROCK AND HEAVY METAL HEROES

SEAN KELLY

DUNDURN
TORONTO

Editor: Allister Thompson
Design: Courtney Horner
Printer: Webcom

Library and Archives Canada Cataloguing in Publication

Kelly, Sean, 1972-
        Metal on ice : tales from Canada's hard rock and heavy metal
heroes / by Sean Kelly.

Issued also in electronic formats.
ISBN 978-1-4597-0709-2

        1. Heavy metal (Music)--Canada. 2. Rock music--Canada.
I. Title.

ML3534.6.K295 2013   782.421660971   C2013-900809-8

1   2   3   4   5   17   16   15   14   13

We acknowledge the support of the **Canada Council for the Arts** and the **Ontario Arts Council** for our publishing program. We also acknowledge the financial support of the **Government of Canada** through the **Canada Book Fund** and **Livres Canada Books**, and the **Government of Ontario** through the **Ontario Book Publishing Tax Credit** and the **Ontario Media Development Corporation**.

Care has been taken to trace the ownership of copyright material used in this book. The author and the publisher welcome any information enabling them to rectify any references or credits in subsequent editions.
                                                                — *J. Kirk Howard, President*

The publisher is not responsible for websites or their content unless they are owned by the publisher.

VISIT US AT

Dundurn.com | @dundurnpress | Facebook.com/dundurnpress | Pinterest.com/dundurnpress

Dundurn
3 Church Street, Suite 500
Toronto, Ontario, Canada
M5E 1M2

Metal on Ice
is dedicated to the hard rock faithful,
the friends I've made on the journey,
and the family that has supported me.

contents

Introduction

RITES OF INITIATION INTO CANADA'S HARD ROCK SCENE

In 1984/85 I was a member of the G&P Welding PeeWee A hockey team in my Northern Ontario home town of North Bay, Ontario. As with most young Canadian boys, there was *nothing* more important than my regular schedule of Tuesday night practices and Friday night games. That all changed with the musical revelations pumping through the speakers of an intimidatingly large ghetto blaster, property of one Scott Dean, the toughest eleven-year-old you'd ever meet. Scott had a penchant for getting into physical altercations with members of the opposing teams, their parents, and sometimes even his own parents. But he also demonstrated a protective sympathy for my own gentle nature, and I could always count on Scott to deliver payback (usually in the form of a crosscheck to the throat or back) to anyone who levelled me on the ice.

The music from Scott's ghetto blaster would pump us up as we rocked out to the strains of Survivor's "Eye of the Tiger," Billy Squier's "The Stroke," and Chilliwack's "My Girl." This was the stuff you could count on hearing every time you strapped on your roller skates and hit the Northern Lights Roller Rink, an aluminium-sided monstrosity that was home to many first kisses, first boob-grabs, and first beatings at the hands of moustachioed pre-adults in cut-off tees, hi-top sneakers, and too-tight jeans. But one day Scott threw on something that pushed the pedal down much *much* harder and a *lot* heavier. It was a band called Helix, and the song was "Rock You." All the familiar elements that used to exist in the background of the music I'd heard (guitars, drums, vocals) for me all of a sudden came screaming into the foreground. Within the first few measures of the tune's famous call-and-response chorus of "Gimme an R (R!), O (O!), C (C!), K (K!) … whatcha got (ROCK) and whatcha gonna do? ROCK YOU!" a shift in perception happened. Music wasn't just going to be a background soundtrack for my life; it was going to *be* my life. I was going to learn to play the guitar for real! I was gonna shout at the devil. I sure as hell wasn't gonna take it, and I *was* gonna rock you.

Thus began my process of discovery of hard rock and heavy metal music. The music was piped into my life in the same way it was for any number of Canadian pre-teens — picked up from the schoolyard and the ever-growing output of music videos airing on the music specialty shows of the day. Shows like *Friday Night Videos*, *Video Hits*, and *Good Rockin' Tonite* played the odd video of the heavy metal I was craving, but my main fix came from the freshly launched MuchMusic channel, and specifically *The Power Hour*, a sixty-minute blast of metal in all its existing incarnations. Helix loomed large in my mind, but to be honest, they were overshadowed by the metal sounds coming from the U.S. and Europe. These bands just seemed to be more prevalent at the time and certainly had more print space in rock and metal rags like *Hit Parader*, *Circus*, *Creem* and whatever other publication I could pick up at Shoppers Drug Mart. Even though the wheels of establishing our Canadian cultural identity had long been set into motion by the mid-1980s, I believe it is safe to say that as consumers of pop culture product, many of us were still largely informed by content coming from south of the border. We modelled the idyllic view of family life on such shows as *The Cosby Show*, *Family Ties*, and *Growing Pains*, marvelled at the Americanized bravado of Indiana Jones and Rocky Balboa, and most definitely consumed much more American music than Canadian. Canada was willing and ready to mainline American entertainment.

As far as music goes, the ever growing popularity of the cable TV medium bombarded us with images of American and European bands performing to screaming throngs of thousands. In doing so, these artists seemed like rock gods who would never deign to play in arenas that held fewer than 10,000 people. In other words, for those of us Canadians who grew up in smaller locales, simple mathematics seemed to dictate that we would *never* see these artists in their perfect natural environment, an eighty-foot stage with a full array of speakers piled high, walls of Marshall cabinets, and enough lights to power a small city. Of course, I was aware that there were Canadian bands out there, but they really only existed in my periphery. I heard their songs on the radio and I had seen their videos. Many of them, like Helix, Kick Axe, and Honeymoon Suite, were definitely contenders for my devotion as a fan. Looking back, I doubt I really considered the fact that they were Canadian at all. They just existed in the shadows of the heavyweights whose image, hype, and music I had been consuming via American mass media.

The musical fare of Quiet Riot, Twisted Sister, Mötley Crüe, and Def Leppard were doing heavy rotation on my parents' archaic turntable, and my hockey-playing buddy Scott and I would spend hours listening then poking away at the out-of-tune second-hand electric guitars we had acquired for Christmas. There was no Internet guitar tablature or YouTube videos to learn from, so instead we perfected the techniques we could master, posing in front of the mirror and smoking cigarettes in the backyard. Scott had long blond hair and looked like an eleven-year-old rock star. And frankly, faking along to records and sneaking out for a smoke in the backyard with a cool-looking kid was satisfying enough. This was gonna be my "thing." I really wasn't prepared for the new dimension my "thing" would take on after I witnessed my first rock 'n roll concert, nor was I aware until years later of the significance of the venue in which it took place.

Any hockey enthusiast who has grown up in Canada has a deeply ingrained sensory perception of their local arena. We can see vividly the colours of the seats that define the sections, the pennants and photos that honour hometown heroes made good, the rickety huts where the programs are sold. The smell of concession stand French fries and vinegar permeate the building, mixing with the scents of sweat and ice. But perhaps the first thing noticed upon entering a rink are the sounds: the slap-back of children's voices against the brick of the foyers, the rattling of the Plexiglas that keeps the crowd safe from flying pucks and broken sticks, and the reverberant echoes of bone-crushing hits against the boards.

By 1985, Memorial Gardens in North Bay had already been host to many memories for me: Ontario Hockey League games courtesy of the North Bay Centennials, the circus, the Harlem Globetrotters, and the odd time when my house league minor hockey teams would be given the chance to play in the "big room." I was aware that the Gardens hosted myriad events, but in my mind the main purpose for its existence was to house hockey in all its various age groupings. That would change for me on a fall night in 1985. My growing passion for hard rock and heavy metal blossomed into a full-blown obsession when I saw a double bill featuring Helix and Honeymoon Suite.

Everything about that first concert was exciting, even picking up the tickets at the Garden's box office weeks before the actual event. The more I stared at the names of the bands on my ticket, the more attention I would pay to their music as it was piped into my bedroom over the airwaves … Helix's "Rock You" was every bit the anthem "Shout at the Devil" or "Rock of Ages" were — hell, maybe even more! And Honeymoon Suite's "New Girl Now" contained the perfect combination of bubblegum melody and crunching guitars. I purchased the records with money saved from allowances and paper routes and dove deeply into the music. These Canadian bands soon moved up the ranks in my eyes to become the equals of their American and European counterparts. And perhaps more importantly, they were coming to bring the rock 'n roll message directly to me, in the most sacred of Canadian venues: the local hockey arena!

The day of the show I pedalled my ten-speed around the arena all day, hoping to catch a glimpse of these rock gods. Sure enough, two tour buses pulled up behind the arena in the afternoon, and one by one the long-haired, leather-clad members of the bands poured out of their respective buses. As I collected autographs and exchanged high-fives and back slaps, it dawned on me that there was a strange and wonderful dichotomy at work here. These musicians were (in my estimation) miles above me in the scale of human existence, far more than mere mortals, and yet here they were treating me with kindness and respect. And not only that, they were *thanking* me for buying their albums and coming to their show! I even got to go into the arena early and watch the crew setting up the show, hanging the lighting rig, and tuning the guitars.

As for the show itself … completely mind-blowing. The familiar reverberations of those arena boards as they absorbed and reflected the blows of crushing drums, piercing Marshall stacks, and soaring vocals echoed in my ears and my heart long after the show ended. The memory of rocking out with my childhood buddies Paul Vaillancourt, Jason Turner, and Russell Hunter (and my older sister Pam and cousin Colleen, our chaperones for the evening) is one I have always kept close to my heart. Yet one poignant moment escaped me and was only brought to my memory on a stop in Edmonton on a recent tour of Canada with Nelly Furtado (with whom I currently play guitar). My friend Paul swears that I turned to him at some point during the show, looked him square in the eyes, and shouted over the din of electric guitars: "I'm gonna be on that stage one day!"

Years later, as I was about to perform with Helix at the 2009 Rocklahoma Festival on a bill with Ratt, Night Ranger, and Warrant on a massive festival stage, I reminded lead singer Brian Vollmer of that concert and the kindness the Helix boys showed me. He didn't remember, but he really didn't need to. I did.

These early musical experiences set me on a course from which I could never turn back, a course which has me writing this very chapter from the Andaz Hotel (formerly the old "Riot Hyatt") on Hollywood's Sunset Strip as I make my living as a professional musician. The road to Canadian musical glory is not lined with the palm trees of this fabled strip or the top-down convertibles I am watching pass by. It is a road slick with black ice, obscured by blizzards, and littered with moose and deer that could cause peril for a band strung out from too little sleep and too much excess as they thunder along the Trans-Canada Highway in a cube van.

Metal on Ice is a look at the pursuit of the Canadian rock 'n roll dream as lived and experienced by a number of musicians who rose to some level of prominence during the eighties and early nineties. It is also a story of the realities of the music business, a look at the nuts and bolts of what went into making the music we have come to know and love. The artists share in their own words their experiences of climbing the rock 'n roll ladder and striving to make a mark both domestically and internationally.

I largely focus on the Canadian bands and artists that helped formulate my own dreams to make a living as a guitar player, and in some cases I have worked with these artists. Almost everyone I talked to for this book based their game plan for a career in music on the models of American and European bands. However, I believe there is a distinct identity in Canadian bands that differentiates them from their U.S. and European counterparts. The musical differences are subjective, but hearing them tell their stories just *feels* Canadian. They also have an edge that comes with a life lived hard in the name of rock 'n roll … kind of like a Tim Hortons coffee spiked with Jack Daniels.

And for purists, don't get too hung up on what constitutes heavy metal in this book. For me, if it was on *The Power Hour,* the guitars were loud, and the hair was long, it was heavy metal, eh? At the end of the day, it really is only rock 'n roll, and I do like it.

In *Metal on Ice*, we get first-hand accounts from early to mid-eighties headbangers like Helix, Kick Axe, Coney Hatch, and Anvil, and rockers who made their mark in the second wave of Canada's big hair daze like Killer Dwarfs, Brighton Rock, Harem Scarem, Slik Toxik, Sven Gali, and Syre. Bands like Honeymoon Suite and Haywire were on the more polished, melodic side of the hard rock spectrum, and bands like Sacrifice, Razor, and Voivod represented the power and speed of thrash — but were their struggles and dreams really all that different? And what about the role of Canadian women in a scene that is often perceived as hyper-macho? Lee Aaron, Darby Mills (Headpins), and Holly Woods (Toronto) brought easily as much power and swagger as the boys who made the noise did, and their story is a big part of the narrative of heavy rock in Canada.

Each chapter of the book will deal with a step in the process that these Canadian hard rock and metal bands went through to bring their music to the masses. And for the record, *Metal on Ice* reads better with some Canadian rock blaring in the background. So turn the page and GIV'ER!

the players

Man, I forget who said it, but it sure is true: writing about music is like dancing about architecture. How the hell can you describe the glorious feeling that washes over a teenager when he hears a perfectly voiced power chord coming out of dimed Marshall stack? What words do justice to the pounding of a double bass drum kit soaked in cathedralesque reverb, or the sound of a singer tearing his or her vocal chords apart reaching for notes that exist only in the upper reaches of Heavy Metal Heaven? It's a futile exercise, but I thought it best in this chapter to frame the work of these artists as I saw, heard, and felt them, because as any good rock musician knows, it is *all* about feel.

When I think about the Canadian heavy metal and hard rock bands that moved me in the eighties, I group them in categories based loosely on era and style. The first group is those influenced by seventies heavy metal and hard rock, British bands like Black Sabbath, Judas Priest, Deep Purple, and Led Zeppelin; Australia's AC/DC; Germany's Scorpions; American bands like Grand Funk Railroad, Vanilla Fudge, Blue Cheer, and Cactus; and Canadian bands like April Wine and Bachman Turner Overdrive: the key foundation elements. No doubt there were other influences, but this gets us in the sonic ballpark.

Helix, Coney Hatch, Anvil, White Wolf, and Kick Axe best represent this first phase to me. Each of these bands first cut their teeth on the Canadian bar scene in the seventies. There are definitely differences in approach between these bands and many subtleties which define each group's style and sound.

Kitchener, Ontario's Helix was the embodiment of approachable, relatable, head bang-able working class heavy metal. They wrote and performed songs custom-made for hockey arenas. Simple and ear-catching, Helix's recorded works reflected an understanding of the musical foundations of the best heavy rock that came before, no doubt learned from their years of pounding it out on the seventies Ontario bar circuit. With Helix, there was always enough AC/DC to keep it tough, enough Van Halen to keep it fun, enough Priest to keep it metal, and enough Zeppelin to keep it grooving. Helix painted with broad strokes and primary sonic colours, but the colours were always concurrent with what was happening with the best of their peers both domestically and internationally at the time of any given release.

After recording and releasing two albums independently via their own H&S label (a partnership with manager William Seip, a guiding force in the development of Helix's look and sound throughout their career), the band made headway with a string of gold and platinum albums on Capitol Records/EMI. *No Rest for the Wicked* (1983), *Walking the Razor's Edge* (1984), *Long Way to Heaven* (1985), and *Wild in the Streets* (1987) are chock full of coliseum-ready rockers fuelled by the golden throat of Brian Vollmer. His voice could cut like a razor blade ("Heavy Metal Love," "Rock You," and "Wild in the Streets") or be power ballad-smooth ("Deep Cuts the Knife," "Make Me Do (Anything You Want)," "Dream On"). Helix put on a highly choreographed live show that was equal parts rock spectacle and acrobatics display, with Vollmer executing daring commando rolls after he plummeted from the top of twenty-five-foot speaker column stacks. As Helix entered headline status on the Long Way to Heaven and Wild in the Streets tours, they put on arena-worthy spectacles replete with ego ramps, massive light trusses, and a drum riser high enough for the entire venue to catch a great view of drummer Greg "Fritz" Hinz's famous "full moons." Guitarist Brent "The Doctor" Doerner's Eddie Van Halen-inspired virtuosity was a great complement to co-axeman Paul Hackman's bluesy style, and Belfast-born bassist Daryl Gray brought a strong Irish tenor and considerable bass and keyboard chops to a band that could step into the ring with any world-class hard rock outfit.

I recall a TV commercial for one of those compilation albums that were really raging back in the eighties. I used to love them because I could get a sampler of all the hits at the time, and every once in a while be thrilled when one of my hard rock favourites made the grade. This commercial was running through videos of the various artists that appeared on the compilation and my head spun around when I heard … "and Canada's Coney Hatch with 'Devil's Deck'!" Once I heard the lines "Harlot Christine, just a kid of sixteen" accompanied by that driving beat and those crunching guitars, another band was added to my favourites list.

The hard rock that Coney Hatch was dealing from that devil's deck came from an interesting set of influences and an even more interesting band dynamic. Vocalist and guitarist Carl Dixon was a student of the great classic rock and soul music of the sixties and seventies. Dixon possesses a near-perfect voice for rock radio, soulful and powerful in range. In highly developed and commercial compositions like "Hey Operator," "Devil's Deck," and "Girl from Last Night's Dream," you can hear the time Dixon spent studying and absorbing classic rock song structure. With bassist and co-vocalist Andy Curran, we get a more angular approach to writing and vocal delivery that is a culmination of new wave and New Wave of British Heavy Metal influences. Curran has a darker, almost spoken vocal approach, one that highlights the more abstract nature of his compositions ("Monkey Bars," "Stand Up," "Shake the Stick"). Complementing the duo lead vocalist approach were guitarist Steve Shelski (a graduate of Toronto's prestigious Humber College Jazz program whose star turn in the solo to "Monkey Bars" has confounded cover band guitarists for years!) and drummer Dave "Thumper" Ketchum, a great four-on-the-floor pounder in the classic hard rock style. Their 1982 self-titled debut album, released on Anthem Records and produced by Kim Mitchell, was a gold-certified smash. Subsequent albums *Outta Hand* (1984) and *Friction* (1985) saw the band refining its sound, bringing in a more AOR and melodic rock sensibility. For the *Friction* record, Ketchum was replaced by Barry Connors (a veteran of the Lee Aaron Band and Toronto). Touring with bands like Iron Maiden and Judas Priest showed Coney Hatch how the big boys did it and in turn helped them establish their own reputation as a live act of the highest order. The Hatch's photogenic good looks kept the girls happy and their heavy duty riffs kept teenage boys dropping their allowance money on Coney Hatch merchandise (you would have been hard pressed to roam the halls of a Canadian high school in the mid-eighties and not run into a few guys sporting Coney Hatch concert jerseys with three-quarter-length sleeves).

Interesting side note: current prog-metal Dream Theater vocalist James Labrie (then known as Kevin) actually replaced Dixon as lead vocalist for a spell during the band's last run in the eighties. I never got to see Coney Hatch back in their heyday, even though I had a ticket to a show at École Secondaire Algonquin, the French high school in North Bay. I can't remember what tour it would have been since I was quite young, and my immaturity only compounded my disappointment when the show was cancelled due to poor ticket sales. I remember the DJ from 600 CFCH, the station sponsoring the show, pleading with the rock community of North Bay to buy a ticket so that the promoters would not be afraid to bring future concerts to the town. I held a grudge against every rock fan in town who didn't buy a ticket. *What a bunch of dicks*, I thought! I wanted so desperately for these bands to come to town, to soak up some of their musical magic in the concert bowl or high school gym, or wherever the hell I could see them! This wouldn't be the last time this kind of disappointment would enter my life.

I was beyond stoked to see that Belleville, Ontario-born Lee Aaron; Regina, Saskatchewan's Kick Axe; and Edmonton, Alberta's White Wolf were teaming up to come to Memorial Gardens for a heavy metal triple bill! I mean, seeing Helix and Honeymoon Suite on a double bill was pretty crazy in its own right, but to see *three* bands in one show, well, this was too much. However, my heart sank as I once again heard my local DJ telling me that this concert, too, was going to be cancelled. While I didn't know it at the time, Kick Axe bassist Victor

Langen years later informed me it was because all of their gear had been impounded by the RCMP after a gig in Winnipeg, thanks to the less than scrupulous business dealings of their manager (who had also fled the country to avoid criminal prosecution). The band managed to limp through the next night's gig in Thunder Bay with pawn shop gear, but it was later decided they were not doing themselves any favours by sounding like a transistor radio. My disappointment at missing yet another concert was met with blank stares by my circle of friends, shrugged shoulders, and the more than occasional "Who the fuck are Kick Axe and White Wolf?" Knuckleheads.

Kick Axe had a sound that was really easy for me to love. When I first heard their gold-certified album *Vices*, I was instantly hooked by a familiar sound. It was the production style of Spencer Proffer, who had signed Kick Axe to his Pasha record imprint. Proffer had helmed the boards for Quiet Riot's mega smash *Metal Health*, the album that really kick-started the appearance of heavy metal and hard rock in the charts. I could hear the trashy, boomy midrange production of that album in *Vices*, but I thought it had *way* better songs. "On the Road to Rock" and "Heavy Metal Shuffle" kicked an inordinate amount of ass. Vocalist George Criston (an American who replaced original singer Gary Langen) was a top-notch metal belter, the guitar team of Larry Gillstrom and Ray Harvey had all the technical proficiency needed to shred in a post-Yngwie Malmsteen hard rock world (as well as the taste to know when to use it!), and the rhythm section of Brian Gillstrom and Victor Langen had the pounding groove necessary to take full advantage of Proffer's booming production. The Kick Axe video for "On the Road to Rock" is mandatory viewing, and Langen's custom-made Fury "Bat" bass guitar is still one of the coolest instruments I've ever seen.

White Wolf were cut from a somewhat similar sonic cloth as Kick Axe, but perhaps a little more Euro — highly melodic but with that 1984 razor-like guitar edge. They had two albums that bothered the lower regions of the U.S. Billboard Top 200, 1984's *Standing Alone* and 1986's *Endangered Species*. White Wolf was led by lead singer Don Wolf (who would later lend his background vocal talents to Poison's multi-platinum *Flesh & Blood* album) and lead guitarist/producer Cam MacLeod, and to my mind they are the best representation of the Teutonic influence of Scorpions or Accept in Canadian metal, particularly on the debut. I really dug the video for "She," which had a bit more of an American sound, or maybe a heavier Aldo Nova-type trip. Oh yeah, I didn't talk to Aldo Nova for this book, but I should probably mention that with his smash hit "Fantasy" he pretty much invented the sound that Jon Bon Jovi would co-opt on "Runaway" and then sell to billions of people. So thank him or hate him for that. Anyway, White Wolf was signed in the U.S. to the RCA label, which was kind of notorious for taking great hard rock bands and burying their careers; thus the suggestion that RCA was an acronym for Recording Cemetery of America.

Lee Aaron had turned up on my radar with her *Lee Aaron Project* and *Metal Queen* albums. To be honest, it wasn't until her 1987 self-titled album and 1989's *Body Rock* that I really got into Aaron's music, but I always loved her voice. Her marketing team was playing up the Heavy Metal Siren sexpot stereotypes pretty hard and heavy, and of course that was of considerable interest to a young lad entering his teens. However, I was way more impressed with the power of her vocals. When Lee sings heavy metal, it sounds like a guitarist with an amazing, really wide, controlled vibrato playing through a tube amp that has been warming up for a few hours … saturated and sweet, with enough dirt and grit to rock and a perfect combination of all the right harmonics. Songs like "Metal Queen," "Whatcha Do to My Body," and "Hands On" (all co-written by Aaron) are undeniably important parts of Canada's heavy rock lexicon.

After watching Sacha Gervasi's documentary *Anvil! The Story of Anvil*, you would think that the band had been a long-suffering and tragically ignored joke, only to taste the fame and glory they so desperately longed for in their golden years. And I guess to the mainstream that is what it looks like. To my young metal sensibilities at the time, they were just another pretty cool Canadian metal band. Hell, they had records out, they went on tour, I saw them on TV … what's to pity about that? In fact, I remember watching a video for their classic track "Metal on Metal," a clip that featured the band performing in front of 80,000 screaming Japanese fans during the 1984 Super Rock festival, and thinking that it was pretty damn cool that a band from Canada could even *get* to Japan, much less play to such a crowd!

Anvil's first three records, particularly the classics *Metal on Metal* (1982) and *Forged in Fire* (1983), are highly influential precursors to the American thrash movement, forging classic heavy metal with moments of intense technical proficiency. In retrospect, you can see the influence that Robb Reiner's drumming had on future skin pounders, and guitarist/vocalist Steve "Lips" Kudlow was a riff-meister *par excellence*. Rounded out by guitarist Dave Alison and bassist Ian Dickson, Anvil looked like a pretty traditional metal band. However, the overt descriptions of sexual practice and deviance in their lyrics really suggested more of a performance art approach, with Lips even bringing a variety of sex toy props into the live performance (any guy who can play a guitar solo with a vibrator and *mean* it is surely working on a different artistic plane!).

I have a not-so-fond recollection of going to see Anvil play at a North Bay bar called Wylder's (named after the fact that it was on Wylde Street and things got wild there, I suppose). This would have been later on in their career, the early nineties. I was always a big fan of their song "Mad Dog" from 1987's *Strength of Steel* album. With a crowd of maybe twenty people in the club, I noticed a band member (not one of the loveable cofounders from the Anvil movie) sitting at the bar. Eager to go talk to someone who was actually involved in the occupation I was hoping to follow, I approached him and asked him if "Mad Dog" was in the set. His response was "If you want to hear that song, go home and listen to the album," and then he turned his back to me. Who knows, maybe the song brought back bad memories for him, or maybe he was having a bad day on the road, but at the time all I could think was *You have twenty people in a club and you treat the one who actually gives a shit like that?* This was the exact opposite of how I felt when I met the Helix and Honeymoon Suite guys at my first concert. I was all ready to hate every minute of Anvil's performance but was converted back into an admirer after witnessing the conviction with which Lips attacked the stage and his material that night. In front of only a handful of people, he delivered a performance worthy of a stadium, and I will always remember that. And you too, grumpy bass player.

A band that kind of straddles the line between being considered an early-to-mid-eighties band and a mid-to-late-eighties band to me is Killer Dwarfs. The Dwarfs technically came up through the late seventies and eighties cover and touring scene, but their most important contributions came in the latter phase. I had seen the video for "Heavy Metal Break-down" (from their self-titled debut on Attic Records) in the early days of the *Power Hour*, and it was most definitely pretty good. But when guitarist Mike Hall and bassist Ronald Mayer joined remaining founding members Russ Graham and Darrell Millar, the sparks really started to fly. The Dwarfs second record, 1986's *Stand Tall*, is truly art imitating life, a rallying cry from a band hell-bent on bringing their music to the people their way, in the face of record company indifference. The standout tracks on the album were the pounding and groovy title track (the video for which shows the band literally making their own records in the most outrageous and hilarious display of the DIY ethic ever committed to film) and "Keep the Spirit Alive," a song that contains one of the greatest melodic hooks in the recorded history of hard rock, aided in no small part by Graham's emotive delivery and a golden guitar progression courtesy of Hall. It is really hard to explain how good it feels to hear Russ Graham sing. In the same way that Helix's "Rock You" set me on my personal heavy metal journey, "Keep the Spirit Alive" was fuel for the tiger in my tank as I continued on my musical path. I really *believed* that Russ believed, and meeting him years later, I could see in his eyes that he did. Killer Dwarfs brought a sense of humour to their stage shows, playing up the diminutive stature of their vocalist by having him ride a tricycle around on stage, pop out of a box, and roll around like a demented schoolboy. But just like the best humour, there was always substance and meaning behind the joke, and Killer Dwarfs had that in spades with albums like 1988's *Big Deal*, 1990's *Dirty Weapons*, and 1992's *Method to the Madness* (an album which featured Newfoundland's greatest rock 'n roll export, Gerry Finn, on lead guitar).

Syre was a band I really only knew of from their two videos, "Say Hi to My Girlfriend" and "In Your Eyes." In a pre-Napster world, our version of enjoying music we hadn't officially purchased was to tape videos on our VHS players and watch them over and over until the tapes wore out. I never actually owned their sole A&M Records release, *It Ain't Pretty Being Easy*, but their reputation as a killer live act on the Canadian bar circuit even made its way to my high school halls. Formed in 1986, this band was one of the best examples of a Canadian hard rock band without pretense or any modus operandi other than to play the shit out of their instruments and have a good time *all* the time. Those people with a loftier philosophical view of music might find this shallow, but Syre, made up of vocalist Doug Weir, drummer Jamie Constant, guitarists Chip Gall and Rick Mead, and bassist Chris Caron, would probably just tell them to relax and have a beer. Syre built their reputation by bringing a stadium-sized attitude to the small clubs they played across Canada, and an ever-growing fanbase of repeat customers was the reward.

Sword was a mid-to-late-eighties period heavy metal band that caught my ears thanks to a storming track called "FTW (Follow the Wheel)" from their 1986 Aquarius Records debut *Metalized*. I absolutely *loved* this track. With a chorus of "Follow the wheel, wheels of fire," what metal-loving teen could resist singing along? To this day, I still don't know if the mix of the singular and plural in that chorus was on purpose, or a result of the Saint-Bruno, Quebec-born and raised Rick Hughes' challenges singing in English, but when it rocks *this* hard, who cares? Sword was devastatingly tight, and the *Metalized* album was a fresh take on the classic NWOBHM influences. Hughes, along with brother Dan on drums, guitarist Mike Plant, and bassist Mike Larocque (how perfect!), led Sword down a musical path that married Iron Maiden, Dio, and Deep Purple influences. This "trad" heavy metal approach carried on with the release of 1988's *Sweet Dreams*. Rick Hughes would later go on to join the hair metal ranks in the early nineties with the band Saints & Sinners, which would release a self-titled album of sleaze rock a-go-go, also on the Aquarius label.

This might be where I lose any credibility I might have had with the metal community, but then again, what could be more metal than not giving a damn?

I have always loved the sounds of keyboards blended with distorted electric guitars. Whether they were used as a special effect, a simple harmonic pad, or a full-on baroque frenzy of notes, I am a big fan of the 88s and the bands that use them. Now, one of the things about keyboards is that the bands that use them tend to lean a little heavier on the melody and a little lighter on the heavy. I argue that when you are watching bands like Haywire, Honeymoon Suite, Brighton Rock, and Harem Scarem pound it out live, there are enough hard rock elements to justify their inclusion in a book on hard rock and metal. Not to mention the fact that they worked the same circuits as most of the other bands in this book anyway!

Niagara Falls-based Honeymoon Suite's hard rock ringer is definitely guitarist Derry Grehan. No matter how poppy an HMS tune might get, Grehan has enough Blackmore and Van Halen-drenched attitude in his playing and his tone to qualify as a genuine hard rock guitar hero. What kid watching the Live Aid broadcast in '85 could forget the Pepsi commercial in which Grehan's searing lead guitar was *sooo* rocking that it could blow the caps off a line-up of cola bottles? For every summer-soaked radio hit ("Wave Babies") or new wave-flavoured tune ("Stay in the Light") on Honeymoon Suite's 1984 debut, there was a riff-heavy rocker to complement it ("New Girl Now," "Burning In Love"). Ray Coburn is a world-class keysman who has treaded the planks with everyone from Dalbello to Kim Mitchell, and he always concocted cool textures that sat perfectly in the mix. Johnny Dee's vocals were pure AOR class, and the rhythm section of drummer Dave Betts and ex-Toronto (the band) bassist Gary Lalonde kept the affair suitably grounded in classic rock synchronicity.

Subsequent albums like 1986's *The Big Prize* and 1988's *Racing After Midnight* kept the pop/hard rock balance going. *Racing After Midnight* really showcased Grehan's Van Halen-esque approach (hey, the album was produced by Van Halen producer Ted Templeman, after all!).

Knowing that Montreal-based journalist, radio personality, and avowed defender and crusader for all things eighties Mitch Lafon was a big fan of HMS, I asked him for an exclusive perspective on this Canadian melodic rock gem.

"Honeymoon Suite was Canada's answer to Van Halen, but with a greater pop sensibility. Guitarist Derry Grehan had the same flair and showmanship as icon Eddie Van Halen, but there was only room for one 'Eddie.' The songs crafted by singer Johnnie Dee had the hooks and the memorable singalong choruses. How could you deny the infectiousness of songs like 'New Girl Now,' 'Feel It Again,' or the tear-jerking balladry of 'What Does It Take'? The band has maintained a presence in Canada for over thirty years now. Sadly, Canadian and international record label politics have kept the band from achieving world domination, but that's fine. Honeymoon Suite remains Canada's confectionery pop secret with massive guitars, gravel vocals, and foot-stomping tunes."

Brighton Rock was another band from the Niagara region (something in the waterfall?) that could keep it heavy and pompy. When I would see videos for songs like "We Came to Rock" and "Can't Wait for the Night" off their 1986 debut *Young, Wild, and Free,* I always felt this was a band that wanted to rock much harder than what was coming across on their recorded work. They had a very manicured image, with really big hair and really shiny clothes, but there was something about the way they wielded those pointy guitars on the screen that suggested there was metal underneath the glossy production sheen. Scottish-born screecher par excellence Gerry McGhee had a gruff but highly melodic vocal style that brought to mind Dan McCafferty of Nazareth, and guitarist Greg Fraser was a master of the whammy bar, swooping in, on, over, and around the notes with perfect intonation. Their second album, *Take a Deep Breath*, went gold thanks to the power ballad "One More Try," but I really dug the single "Hangin' High and Dry." These guys could really rock an anthem, and I always loved their stacked vocal harmonies. By the time Brighton Rock hit 1991's *Love Machine* album the band had lost the keyboards and had moved on to a drier, guitar-driven sound that was more in line with their live show. But I kinda missed those keyboards!

Okay, let's talk about Prince Edward Island's Haywire. On their 1986 debut *Bad Boys* they came across as anything but. Videos for the tracks "Bad Bad Boy" and "Standin' In Line" had way too many eighties sweaters hanging off one shoulder, too much hand dancing without instruments, and generally too much new wave pop influence to be considered hard rock. But once again, in guitarist Marvin Birt I *felt* a hard rock guitar hero waiting to bust out of his pop confines and lay down some molten metal licks! He hinted at it in the solo for "Standin' in Line," something in the way he delivered his whammy bar-scooped, palm-muted licks as he stared down the camera.

Haywire's closeted hard rock tendencies were further revealed on 1987's *Don't Just Stand There.* The tunes were still pretty poppy, and in the case of massive hit "Dance Desire," downright funky. But Birt was pinching the harmonics a little harder on his guitar and the solos were becoming a little more fleet of finger. Lead singer Paul MacAusland's mane was getting a little longer, drummer Sean Kilbride was now rocking a double kick drum set-up, and even the perpetual smiles of keyboardist David Rashed and bassist Ronnie Switzer had a bit more attitude, and there was more leather involved in the look. I saw Haywire open for Helix on the latter's Wild in the Streets tour, and the band came out with fully sanctioned hard rock swagger. I didn't see the band from those early videos who wore pastel sweaters while they danced on cars and shared French fries with their cute teenage girlfriends at some PEI roller rink. I saw a kick-ass rock 'n roll band bringing it down arena-rock style. By the time of 1991's *Nuthouse* album, Haywire was in my eyes a hard rock band. Check out the down 'n dirty shuffle of the first single, "Short End of a Wishbone," for proof.

I remember getting hipped to the band Harem Scarem by my friend and sometimes bandmate Jeff Van Dusseldorp (a keyboard player, go figure). Jeff was already out on the road, living the rock 'n roll dream in a pro outfit called Down 'n Dirty (named after a song by U.S. band Autograph). He was home from a break in the touring schedule, and as we were driving around in his truck he popped in Harem Scarem's self-titled debut. A glance at the artwork showed an outfit with the requisite look of a band who had come of age in the late eighties: big hair, flowing pirate shirts, etc. I was always so impressed that a band from Ontario could look as slick and polished as the American bands. But it was the music that really blew me away. These songs had more hooks than a tackle box, absolutely *huge* harmonies, and the lead guitarist Pete Lesperance was (and still is) a *monster* player. Lead vocalist Harry Hess had one of those voices that just sat perfectly on the radio, really rich and broad-sounding in any range. Jeff and I would drive around in his truck and practise our harmonies to the entire record, picking out choice parts to sing at full blast. Hell, you couldn't help but feel great as you launched into the choruses of "Slowly Slipping Away" and "Hard to Love." When I saw Harem Scarem live in a bar in Oakville, Ontario that summer, I was impressed by how they delivered their polished sound live. The drummer, Darren Smith, just exuded rock star charm and personality, and I would later discover he was also a very talented lead singer and guitar player. He grooved hard with bassist Mike Gionet. They managed to transform the very suburban sports bar they were playing into a real concert experience, with nothing but their music and performance chops. I was going to have to get my shit together as a player if I was going to compete on *this* level.

When I first moved to Toronto in 1991 to study classical guitar at the University of Toronto (but really to try to become a rock star!), hair metal permeated the Yonge Street strip, and the bands that captured the affections of the ladies, the admiration of the guys, and the jealousy of their unsigned competitors were Slik Toxik, Sven Gali, and Big House. The first cassette I purchased when I moved to Toronto was Slik Toxik's *Smooth and Deadly* EP, a teaser to their major label debut *Doin' the Nasty*. This EP, more so than any collection of music I have purchased before or since, really resonated with me as a young musician. Slik Toxik really *sounded* the way Toronto *felt* at the time to me. It was loud and fast-moving, but there was also an undercurrent of sleaze. The lead track was "Big Fuckin' Deal," all about the pursuit of a record deal, which was exactly what I hoped to attain, playing music that sounded a lot like Slik Toxik. Mind you, the music I was writing was nowhere near as good as what ST vocalist/writer Nick Walsh was coming up with, but it was where I wanted to go.

In the same year, I heard what I still consider to be the best Canadian hard rock song of all time, "Dollar in My Pocket (Pretty Things)" by Edmonton band Big House. Vocalist Jan Ek had a lot more attitude than technique in his vocal approach, but *what* an attitude. His tone was so raunchy and authentic, and he just dripped style. I'm sure the fact that Big House started life as a punk band played a huge part in the real rock 'n roll feel in their songs. It was much less precious and perfect than some of their hair metal contemporaries. Guitarist K.B. Broc crafted some of my favourite Canadian rock guitar solos, half Randy Rhoads, half Chuck Berry and 100% awesome! Unfortunately, finding a member of Big House to talk to for this book proved harder than finding a copy of their self-titled album on a record store shelf after 1994!

When Slik Toxik's *Doin' The Nasty* dropped in 1992, the lead single "Helluvatime" came firing out of the gates with a world-class video and one of the best updates on Aerosmith's *Rocks* album sound I'd ever heard. I think what really made this album for me was the fact that I could hear how much Walsh loved all types of hard rock and metal. There were elements of Queensrÿche, L.A. Guns, W.A.S.P., and pretty much everything I had in my own record collection. Seeing Slik Toxik play a packed club show at the Spectrum on Danforth Avenue in Toronto made me realize how much better I was going to have to get in order to cut it in this town. The same thing happened later that year when I heard Sven Gali's debut and saw them blow the roof off the RPM club. "Under the Influence" was the first single and video I saw, and I clearly remember revelling in the power riffs punched out by guitarists Dee Cernile and Andy Frank. Vocalist Dave Wanless was an imposing powerhouse of a frontman, not the usual androgynous skin-and-bones rag doll you might associate with lead singers. Each video and single that followed from the album got me more and more excited for the future of Canadian hard rock and heavy metal, because hey, this type of music was here to *stay*, right?

So these were the bands that I had first-hand, personal experience with, but they are not the only artists I talked to for this book. I wanted to touch on the experiences of thrash metal bands like Razor, Sacrifice, and Voivod. These bands represented the faster, heavier side of metal, and along with Exciter, Annihilator, Varga, and Slaughter made up what my buddy and *Brave Words and Bloody Knuckles* head honcho Metal Tim Henderson describes "an underground of aggressive, fist-pumping ferociousness." They infused the classic sounds of Judas Priest, Iron Maiden, and the New Wave of British Heavy Metal bands like Diamond Head, Saxon, and Motörhead with punk influences, creating a street-level sound that was perfect for picking gravel out of your skin after a nasty skateboard wipeout. Songs like Razor's "Evil Invaders," Sacrifice's "Reanimation," and Voivod's "Ripping Headaches" fascinated me with their sheer relentlessness, and in recent years I have grown to appreciate the technicality and musical intricacy that these bands evinced.

I also wanted the perspective of pioneers like Toronto and Headpins, specifically from Anne "Holly" Woods and Darby Mills, whose strong female presence was felt by thousands of hard rock fans across Canada.

So now that we know who we are talking about, let's find out why we are talking about them. There was a path they needed to take to get from being in the crowd to being on the stage, from being the one who receives the sound to the one who produces and delivers it. Before you get there, you gotta get inspired....

ROCK 'N ROLL VOCATIONS: THE CALL TO ARMS

Has there ever been a proper job description for the "rock star" occupation? I have heard a lot of musicians describe themselves as such. I have heard people say they want to sleep with one, and I have heard many young urban professionals and frat boys claim to party like one. But what drives someone to become an actual rock star, someone who can fully commit to the larger-than-life persona and the hours of dedication it takes to be a world-class performer, writer, musician, and road warrior?

Like all childhood career aspirations, the initial motives are pretty pure. It all comes down to the feeling you get when you hear your first power chord or your reaction to a song that drives you to play it over and over again, soaking in every word, every beat, every piece of studio-created affectation. And sure, seeing the rewards (real or imagined) that come with the ability to create the grooves that rock the world is pretty alluring as well. But the commitment required to really understand a musical instrument to the point of being able to make emotions out of sonics requires something a whole lot more substantive than just a lust for a certain lifestyle. It comes from a quest for the sound.

For a kid wanting to be part of making the multi-layered orgasmic roar of a world-class rock band, a few things need to happen. It's kinda like hockey. Some might know exactly which position they want to play right away and others may need to try out a few before finding where they fit. In music, you gotta choose your instrument, which in turn defines your position in the band. For me, it was a thirty-five-dollar second-hand hollowbody electric guitar my dad got me at a flea market for Christmas. I had no doubts I wanted to be a right winger on the ice, and I had no doubts I wanted to rock an electric guitar on the stage!

For St. Catharines, Ontario's Dermot Fergus Grehan, more famously known as "Derry," guitarist and songwriter for Honeymoon Suite, music entered his life through the rigours of classical training at the behest of his father.

"He was a doctor, and he was into classical and played classical piano every night. We had a stiff Irish Catholic upbringing, and he forced us all into piano lessons. We didn't like it at first, but I took the lessons, Conservatory and all that. When I was about ten or eleven years old, I was walking through Kmart and I was going by the record department and heard Deep Purple's 'Smoke on the Water.' I thought it was the coolest song I ever heard! So I went home and asked my parents if they would let me play guitar, and the deal was, as long as you keep up your piano lessons we'll get you a guitar. I was just coming of age, just becoming aware of Jimi Hendrix and Led Zeppelin and Santana and rock and how cool it was to play guitar. You can't jump around with a piano. It's infinitely cooler wearing a guitar, you know? [laughs]"

The next step is to find other people who want to roar in the same way, and for Victor Langen of Regina, Saskatchewan's Kick Axe, it all started with an iconic 1967 television moment.

"I was changed forever seeing The Who perform on *The Smothers Brothers Comedy Hour*, when Keith Moon used a stick of dynamite to blow up his drums and Pete Townshend pushed over his amp stack. Roger Daltrey was swinging his mic over his head, and all the while John Entwistle just stood there, perfectly still! In that moment, I wanted to be Keith Moon! That started us as kids playing school dances, backyard parties, garages, and basements. We were inspired by Grand Funk Railroad, Mountain, Aerosmith, The Guess Who, April Wine, Rush, Zeppelin, Humble Pie, and Uriah Heep. Kick Axe was initially comprised of classmates and neighbours from Regina. Our goal was to live the rock 'n roll life and do a job we loved in the process."

Nick Walsh from Toronto's Slik Toxik took inspiration from the Canadian artists that arose in the wave before his band stormed the charts in the early nineties.

"Helix was an inspiration, for one. *No Rest for the Wicked*. When I first heard that song 'Does a Fool Ever Learn,' I was like, 'Who is this?' But one of the bands that really stood out for me that not a lot of people know is Kick Axe. That album *Vices*, that song 'Heavy Metal Shuffle,' 'Dreaming About You,' this was great songwriting, great musicianship. George Criston was an excellent singer. That band really, really did it for me, but I mean there was a wave before that. There were bands like Prism. When *Spaceship Superstar* came out when I was only seven or eight years old, that was the coolest thing, and in fact the two things that got me into wanting to be a musician were (a) the KISS *Alive* album cover, and (b) the band BTO. Their songs were so heavy, you know what I mean? Like [singing] 'ride, ride, ride, won't you let it ride.' That was the heaviest stuff I'd ever heard and I was only, like, four years old, so yeah, Canadian rock really influenced me but in the sixties and the seventies there was [basically] no border between Canada and America. There was no border at all. And it was like, whether it was Neil Young or Rick James or Buffalo Springfield and all these bands and actors and so forth, they all did their thing together, Canadians and Americans. And Canada didn't have CanCon [Canadian content regulations], they actually played Canadian music because it was good [laughs]. It wasn't like something that was an added bonus because we're all weak and inferior."

If you were to do a basic summation and description of what a heavy metal or hard rock band line-up looks like, a clichéd list of points might run down as follows:

Lead Singer: Lion-maned vocalist, cocky, blessed with a vocal range that reaches the stratosphere (perhaps aided by unfailingly tight trousers), possesses an ability to charm even the most volatile of crowds with witty repartee or a unison call to arms (e.g. "I hear there's a rock 'n roll PARTAY going on in Mattawa TOOONIIIIIITE!), has an uncanny ability to access food, shelter, and other comforts on the road thanks to sexual magnetism.

Guitarist(s): Fleet of finger, the frontman's (or woman's) onstage foil, often backlit by the glow of power tubes from a wall of Marshall amplifiers and a refrigerator-sized effects rack. Enjoys many of the same proclivities as the lead singer but sometimes has to compensate for lack of vocal range with wild, shredding guitar solos and sheer volume. Often considered the virtuoso of the group.

Bassist: Not often considered the virtuoso of the group, often viewed as the defenceman on the team, keeping things musically safe with simple, pounding grooves that allow the lead singer and guitarist to hog the musical spotlight. Often has to justify his/her function to listeners in a recording situation ("You can't *really* hear what I'm doing, but you'd miss it if it wasn't there").

Drummer: Likes to hit things and make loud noises. Provides necessary percussion solos at heavy metal concerts so that patrons can hit the bar and/or concession stands and also provides an opportunity for the lead singer, guitarist, and bassist to take a piss after consuming all that beer during the first half of the concert. A good drummer can transform a mediocre band into a grinding, driving metal machine that keeps the fists pumping in the air all night long. A bad drummer usually has a van, a PA, or lets the band rehearse at his/her house.

Keyboards: Optional, hated by 90 percent of male metal fans, loved by 90 percent of female metal fans. Often were enlisted to make hard rock music more palatable for radio. Usually classically trained and slumming it in a metal band because all of the good new wave bands already had three keyboard players.

All right, so that is the smartass version, but you could pretty much expect to find some combination of that line-up in a hard rock or metal band in the eighties. The line-ups of these bands were formed and forged in a shared love of the music that came before them.

It has been said that heavy metal is the music of misfits, for people who have a hard time finding their place amongst their peer groups. There is an escapist quality to the music that can make someone society has made to feel small somehow feel larger than life. I know from my own personal experience there was definitely a feeling of social confidence in being a part of a group of musicians who connected with the emotions experienced through playing music. This confidence grew with the mastery of every riff or lick, and with every song performed from beginning to end in a relatively smooth manner.

It's hard to imagine Helix's lead vocalist Brian Vollmer ever lacking in confidence, but it turns out that rock 'n roll was a means of forging his early identity. While his first influence was Johnny Cash, he was later moved by the sounds of Canadian bands like The Guess Who and Steppenwolf (and their German-born singer John Kay). "I was into whisky-throated rock 'n roll singers, and anything I could pick up on CJOY radio out of London, Ontario. I remember I was very into certain songs, like 'Signs' by Five Man Electrical Band, and 'Joy to the World' by Three Dog Night. I think [singing] was the only thing I realized that I could do half-ass well when I was a kid, and it drew attention to me. I was an overweight kid with acne, and I didn't have many friends. I lived out on a farm, I was kind of socially backward, and I realized that when I sang it suddenly drew positive attention to me."

Vollmer, a proud and vocal Canadian to this day, would actively seek out Canadian artists and support them. "I was just a very proud Canadian kid. I was very much into Canada."

Like many kids coming of age in the 1960s, Carl Dixon of Toronto's Coney Hatch found inspiration in the classic sounds of The Beatles, Creedence Clearwater Revival, The Rolling Stones, The Guess Who (which he would later front in place of departed singer Burton Cummings), and Motown. As heavier, guitar-driven music took hold in the seventies, Dixon was swayed by Free, Humble Pie, Deep Purple, Johnny Winter, and other rockers. This love of all things rockin', rollin', and swingin' led Dixon down the career path of professional musician, hooking up with a number of professional travelling bands that toured extensively through Ontario, Quebec, and the Atlantic provinces. He eventually relocated to Montreal and joined the band Firefly, which represented a step up the professional ladder by way of strong players and singers, a reputable booking agent … and a school bus. Still, Ontario called, and Carl returned to Toronto. But what was the motivation for hooking up with the already formed Coney Hatch?

"I needed a job [laughs]. I had felt like Montreal wasn't in the loop if you were an ambitious musician at that time and I started to miss home. The dynamic in the band was changing, and I moved back to stay with my parents in Barrie for a month or so in January and February of 1981. I then started, as you did then, watching Section 635 in the *Toronto Star* classifieds for 'Dramatic and Musical Talent.' There used to be quite a listing every day, especially on the weekends, for bands looking for singers, roadies, bass players, drummers, lots of ads in that section every day. I watched those and called a couple, but one ad jumped out at me: 'Steady working band with management seeks guitar-playing singer.' So I called it and was told to show up at the New Shamrock Hotel at the corner of Coxwell Avenue and Gerrard Street. That's where I went to see Coney Hatch for the first time. Their manager met me there and we sat and watched. They had the strangest collection of original songs that I had ever heard! But what impressed me was that they *had* original songs, probably eight or ten in the show at that time, as well as a lot of AC/DC, and they played Frank Zappa's 'Crew Slut,' The Police's 'Walking on the Moon,' and Van Halen's 'And the Cradle Will Rock.' They shared the vocals around three ways at that time, because that was the old rule, of course, everybody had to pitch in so one singer didn't get too tired."

A successful audition saw Dixon becoming the fourth and final piece of the puzzle that would make up Coney Hatch's line-up for their first two albums.

Toronto, Ontario's Steve "Lips" Kudlow began playing guitar early on in life and at the ripe old age of ten made the decision that music was what he was going to do for a living. After finding a musical synergy with drummer Robb Reiner through their shared love of seventies hard rock giants like Deep Purple, Black Sabbath, Cactus, and Vanilla Fudge, Lips took out an ad in the *Toronto Star*'s Section 635 seeking players for his musical project. However, in an early display of economic caginess, the band had a creative solution for taking care of the matter of the bill for placing the ad.

"We said that whoever wrote the ad put the wrong phone number on it, so we didn't pay for it [laughs]. What are you gonna do, man? We were seventeen, eighteen years old! I don't know … you do whatever it takes to get something done, you know?"

At the dawn of the eighties, in Saint-Bruno, Quebec, two brothers by the name of Rick and Dan Hughes were inspired by a cinematic showing of Led Zeppelin's famed celluloid rock 'n roll odyssey, *The Song Remains the Same*. Seeing the movie was the genesis of their powerhouse metal act Sword.

"That day our lives changed, seriously. At sixteen years old, I wanted to become Robert Plant, and Dan, who was a big guy, he became a drummer. I mean, what drummer is there in the rock genre other than John Bonham? He's right at the top with Keith Moon. We had jobs, but we needed something to hang from the top of the world, and music became that for us. See, my brother and I, we bought drums, and it usually starts out that way, you look in the paper. In the eighties there was no Internet, so if you wanted to buy used equipment you bought the paper and looked in the musician's classifieds! I already had a guitar and amp, so we started to jam, and we heard about Mike Laroque and Mike Plante. Those guys first started out as a KISS tribute band. They were, like, fourteen years old. I mean, those guys were really hot back in Saint-Bruno! Sword was formed at a McDonalds. We were having French fries and they came in to buy something. We said, 'So come here and sit down,' and that's the way Sword was formed, just by chatting there that day at McDonalds. I think the week after that they were at our house and we were having our first jam session."

Two other music-loving siblings hailing from Quebec were the Drover Brothers, Glen (guitar) and Shawn (drums). At one point both brothers served in the ranks of Dave Mustaine's legendary group Megadeth, with Glen joining first and ultimately recommending his brother for the gig when the drum chair opened up (Shawn remains in Megadeth to this day, Glen having left in January of 2008). Previous to Megadeth, the Drovers formed the core of Metal Blade recording artists Eidolon, during which time Glen moonlighted with King Diamond of Denmark's Mercyful Fate. Glen has most recently been called upon to play guitar in Geoff Tate's version of the progressive metal group Queensrÿche. All of the above-mentioned acts require a guitar player who is both digitally agile and firmly dedicated to the art.

So Glen, why the guitar?

"Jeez, I don't know ... I guess I just gravitated to it. My older brother, Brian, played guitar in the seventies, he used to play in a band. He was more of an acoustic player, you know? So there was always an acoustic guitar lying around. So from a very young age I was into music. I think I got my first KISS album when I was six or seven. I was really drawn to music in general, and he had this acoustic guitar lying around. I'd pick it up and start banging away on it, and one day I asked him if he could show me a couple of things. It kind of went from there."

And what motivated the Drovers to go after music as a profession?

"Just a lot of music. I speak for me and Shawn because we started doing all this together, really. We started playing in bands when we were young, in our late teens, playing in bars and all that, playing covers. And then we got into doing recording and stuff like that in the nineties. Once I started getting into the recording end of things it really started to move into a faster gear."

I am always curious, when I see a Canadian musician playing with an established American band, as to what Canadian influences they are bringing to the musical table. In Glen Drover's case, they mirror the progressive path his own playing has taken.

"As a musician, Max Webster would probably be the biggest one. Rush, of course. Saga. Stuff like that. Kim Mitchell definitely, or Max Webster rather, so I'm a huge fan, you know, I listened to that stuff all the time. It's the stuff I grew up with and am very close to."

Voivod is undoubtedly Quebec's most famous heavy metal outfit. Michel "Away" Langevin's motivations for bringing these titans of thrash together were born of a love for a wide variety of music.

"Well, really, it's my love for music, actually. Mainly hard rock, since I was a kid. I started with KISS — my very first band was The Beatles when I was ten or something, but I soon jumped to riff rock, you know? KISS, Alice Cooper, Ted Nugent, and some Canadian rock. April Wine, Triumph, Rush, of course. But it was when the New Wave of British Heavy Metal showed up in 1980 that I really, really got interested. Especially when I heard the first Iron Maiden album. I thought it combined all the elements I really liked in music — heavy metal, punk, progressive rock, Goth music, and so I thought it'd be very cool if I could do that, but it seemed at that time a bit impossible because we lived way up north in French Canada in Jonquière, Quebec, about 300 miles north of Montreal. So it was a long shot for us. In Jonquière, there is the biggest aluminum factory in North America, Alcan. There are also paper mills and all the factories surrounding, and the cold weather and snow, I believe, had an influence on our sound and music."

Fellow thrashers Razor took their inspiration from the heavier side of the spectrum, as well as from their Canadian contemporaries, explains Mike Campagnolo.

"We used to listen to a lot of early hard rock/heavy metal as far back as I can remember, classic stuff like Priest and Sabbath. I remember hearing Motörhead and early Iron Maiden and just freaking out! We'd go down to Record Peddler, a popular Toronto record store, and be checking out the latest music from all over the place. We loved the high energy of bands like Raven, Saxon, and Tank, and Canadian bands like Anvil and Exciter were bursting out on the scene, and it was also the first time I heard demos by Sacrifice and Slaughter [The Canadian thrash band, not the U.S. hair metal band]."

"Our primary influences were Venom, Slayer, Metallica, Mercyful Fate," says Sacrifice guitarist and vocalist Rob Urbinati. "Rush was huge for us. Exciter and Anvil were some Canadian metal bands we looked up to, but local Toronto hardcore band Direct Action was probably more influential. We wanted to go a step further than the Canuck metal bands at the time, and the hardcore bands seemed to be more like us. We liked the aggression and speed but also the fact that punk bands weren't as pretentious and didn't behave like rock stars. They just looked like everyone else in front of the stage. After they played, they weren't hiding backstage — they didn't need to."

A young Harry Hess put his youthful music prodigiousness to an early professional test when he formed the band Blind Vengeance at the tender age of fifteen. That band soon signed to Attic Records and released one record that, according to Hess, "didn't really work out that great with regard to selling and all the things that go along with whatever success is." Already a veteran of the recording industry's circle of life at age eighteen, Hess went on to study at Fanshawe College in London, Ontario, where he took the Music Industry Arts Program. With the experience garnered at the school, Hess set about the task of writing and demoing his own songs, honing his craft and ultimately putting together the band Harem Scarem around his newly refined compositions.

"We were kind of based between the Ajax-Oshawa-Pickering-Whitby area [suburbs of Toronto]. I think I was living in Bowmanville or New-castle at the time, where I had my studio, and so we just had a circle of friends that followed us around in the beginning, and that's how it really started. In the first year as Harem Scarem we focused on the writing and recording side of it, so we didn't do a whole lot of playing, but I would say yeah, maybe like eight months or a year into it, we really started to play a lot. We were doing the regular scene back then, which could have been anywhere from The Gasworks [Toronto metal club] to … we hit all the places, I mean, I would probably be hard pressed to remember all the names of the clubs in the local scene, but as an unsigned band we basically stayed around southern Ontario. I believe we went as far as Windsor [a city near Detroit]."

And what were the influences for a young man who landed his first record deal in his early teens, and who would then chart a course that would see him in control of the production of his band's future recordings?

"I loved Queen and I grew up kind of trying to do that thing. Vocally I was always into bands that had tons of vocal harmonies and big pro-ductions, so at the time I was a giant fan of Mutt Lange and anything he did. All those larger-than-life productions were really my inspiration with regard to recording and writing and just how to go about making records. There were some American influences too, but a lot of it was British, I would say. I don't know if I ever really could say that I loved Mötley Crüe or Poison or any of those bands. I was much more into more production-oriented bands as opposed to what would be consid-ered the glam rock of the time, like Ratt and Poison."

For Doug Weir of London, Ontario's Syre, it was a combination of art and social motivations that saw him get into the music business.

"I always had the desire to create, so music was an excellent outlet … girls seemed to like musicians too! The first band I saw live was [Toronto power-pop band] Goddo at Nathan Phillips Square in Toronto, and I've been a huge fan ever since. One of the great things about being a musician is that, if you're successful, many times you get to meet your musical heroes. I've met and hung out with Goddo through the years and always feel a little star-struck because of my early experiences as a fan. I was also a big Alice Cooper fan. Cooper brought theatrics to rock music and didn't just stand around onstage. This motivated me in later years to put on a bit of a show. The other guys in Syre had a wide variety of favourites, AC/DC, The Sweet, Mott the Hoople, and some good Canadian acts in there, Kick Axe and Headpins and stuff."

Sven Gali's Andy Frank just kind of slid into a music career. "It wasn't really a conscious decision. I started playing guitar and just met a couple of guys and we played a gig in high school and it was like 'Wow, this is great!' We would play at parties and meet girls and then you're thinking *Well, this is a nice way to spend your time!* It certainly wasn't this calling to be creative with my instrument or anything, it really wasn't. I think it was different for Dee [Cernile, Sven Gali's late lead guitarist]; guitar was his life. It was everything he did. In '87 when we got together we were listening to Ratt, Mötley Crüe, Scorpions, Aerosmith and stuff like that. I think for songwriting also, The Beatles. Anybody who writes music, you have to start with The Beatles."

And while Frank did listen to Canadian bands like Coney Hatch, Helix, and Anvil, he also felt a different attitude towards those bands.

"Yeah, I would have considered them different. There certainly was this *thing* about being Canadian. I think there was a clear distinction, whether you were big in Canada or big in other places as well. We thought of them as Canadian bands, but just awesome as well."

Daryl Gray, bassist for Kitchener, Ontario-based Helix, is an Irish immigrant who cut his teeth both in his homeland and later in Canada. For Gray (who actually moved to Canada from Ireland twice, once as a baby of less than a year, to return at the age of five; the second time as a sixteen-year-old) the music of his homeland was a particularly strong guiding force.

"Thin Lizzy was definitely an influence, and another Irish band by the name of Horslips. They were kind of like traditional Irish meets Led Zeppelin, somewhere in between, a clash of the cultures. Also, all the seventies English bands like Slade, Sweet, the main rock bands like Led Zeppelin and Black Sabbath, and a Welsh band named Budgie that I really liked. There was just a whole hodgepodge of different musical influences."

And did Canadian bands make an impact on Gray as a teenager in Ireland?

"The one that I can think of would be Bachman Turner Overdrive. They had 'Taking Care of Business.' They hadn't really had a big influence over there, but 'You Ain't Seen Nothing Yet' was a big hit."

Within a few days of his return to Canada, Gray's new friends set about the business of hipping him to the latest in Canadian rock.

"They introduced me to April Wine, then played me 'Oowatanite,' and I thought, *That's a great song, why haven't I heard it before*? And then they introduced me to another Canadian band, Rush. I thought they sounded a lot like Budgie, and I was thinking at the time I still kind of liked Budgie better. Of course, as I got more exposure to Rush, I listened to *2112* and thought it was brilliant!"

Backtracking a few years, Gray recalls his first experience with an unwieldy guitar and his first foray into the spotlight.

"My first experience trying to put a band together was in Ireland. I would have been about fourteen. I had gotten a guitar when I was thirteen and it really was one of those meat slicers, the action was so high that my fingers really did bleed. And eventually I did upgrade to a real guitar. So I was playing guitar, one of my friends was playing guitar, and we had another guy that was starting off. At school lunch breaks they would have some sort of entertainment, so we got up and played some Status Quo songs and from that I thought, *Okay, well I can handle this, this is pretty cool!*"

Upon getting involved in the music scene in Canada, Gray found that there were similarities between Canada and Europe in terms of vocational challenges.

"The growing pains were similar, just trying to find people who had commitment, talent, and staying power, because there's a lot of great musicians out there but they're committed to going to work in the factory, they're committed to money, they're not committed to making music. That was the same in both countries. The first real band I was in in Canada had a drummer by the name of Greg Critchley, who many years later had moved on to bigger and better things, and the other guys decided that they wanted a steady nine to five … and this was about two weeks before we were to leave for our first tour! That was a band called Nitro. We had our first tour booked by Steve Prendergast through an agency out of Hamilton, who ended up being the manager of Honeymoon Suite."

Another rocker from across the pond who found his rock 'n roll footing in Canada was Gerry McGhee, lead vocalist for Niagara Falls melodic rockers Brighton Rock.

"I grew up in a family with two brothers, sixteen and fourteen years older than me, and we moved here from Scotland. They were always into music so I was always getting to hear Elvis and The Beatles, King Crimson, Zeppelin, Black Sabbath, Paul McCartney, and everything in between, so there was always music in the house. From a really young age all I really wanted to do growing up and watching my idols was sing, so I think I got in my first band when I was about thirteen. I went full-time professional when I was sixteen and played in a couple of bands that did the Northern Ontario and Quebec circuit and all that until I actually returned to the UK, because a band there asked me to come over and join them. At that point it was either you moved to Los Angeles or you moved to London, and I went to London. It didn't work out with the band over there but I learned a lot as far as how dedicated these guys were. They all had day jobs and basically every night they would get together in a little rehearsal area, and they would do nothing but write songs, and I realized that was the key. I realized if I was going to come back here [Canada] it was a waste of time to do anything other than get into your own material if you wanted to make a career out of it. I didn't want to be slugging it out in the bars, six sets a night, seven days a week for the rest of my life."

As would become evident, these very bars that McGhee did not want to spend the rest of his life in would be the connection between many bands and their fans across Canada. But if the rock 'n roll cover circuit was not the be-all and end-all of a music career, what was the ultimate goal for these artists?

"At a young age, it was definitely world domination [laughs]," says Nicholas Walsh, lead vocalist and visionary for Toronto's Slik Toxik. "Getting signed to a record deal was what we were all striving for back then. Without the Internet the only way to make any sort of noise was through the commercial marketing outlets that seemed to be run by record labels."

"Getting signed to a recording contract was a prime goal for the band," says Langen. "The ultimate goal was to live the rock 'n roll life, loving what you do … we hoped that through a record deal, we would get the chance to live our dreams, playing music for a living."

Through signing a contract with a record company, a young band hoped to receive funding to record their album, have the record promoted and distributed through the company's channels and relationships, and also to receive financial support for their touring endeavours.

"Ultimately, the main goal was to demo some songs and get a record deal," says Grehan. "That was back in the days when everybody was trying to get 'The Deal.' The whole business was different then, [the goal being] to get signed."

Weir agrees. "Yes, signing a record contract was important to us. We'd have a wider platform to promote our music through a deal. It was a means to being successful and having a wider touring platform."

Drover adds, "That is one of the big goals, being signed to a label and being able to record an album and present it, and have all the financial support and promotion and everything else that falls under a label. It was definitely a priority, a goal that every band has, I think … if they take themselves seriously."

"Getting signed was the main thing in those days," confirms McGhee.

For Lips Kudlow, a record deal was just one piece of a puzzle that would see him fulfill what some might consider a loftier ambition.

"To put a band together that would never sell out and last pretty much forever, so I kind of did what I was hoping to do [laughs]. The integrity of the sound of the band was really important. I couldn't stand when my favourite band would get watered down just so they could get on the radio. I really, really … ugh."

In Dixon's case, focused goals only become such in the light of the activity that surrounded the band as it drew attention.

"I think we could have done with more discussion about that sort of thing. We didn't really have … it all happened so fast. We knew, 'Yeah, we'd like a record deal. Yeah, we'd like to be on big shows. Yeah, we'd like to be on the radio.' But we only had a vague idea of how that would happen when I joined the band. We all just knew that you write songs and without that you don't stand a chance, so we really got on that path and it all clicked to the point where within six months of me jointing Coney Hatch we had signed a record deal. As I say in my own book, that first year with Coney Hatch was just like a rocket ride. I got on the rocket and then it just took off and it was almost like a movie script where the four scruffy young guys just stumble together and it's the right combination and off they go. I think if we'd had more of an articulated goal we might have been able to weather some of the uncertainties that followed."

"Did we have an ultimate goal in mind? Probably not," says Russ Dwarf, vocalist for Oshawa, Ontario's Killer Dwarfs. "I think we knew we wanted to make our own music. We wanted to make a record, right? Everybody wanted to have a record back then, you know what I mean? And it wasn't like today where you go to Long and McQuade [a Canadian musical instrument retailer] and buy ten thousand dollars' worth of gear and go into your basement and the next thing you know you're on iTunes the next day. It was an actual process where you had to try to get signed."

I often wondered what it was like for musicians from Canada's East Coast in this era to try to stake out a career in the national and international hard rock and metal scene. For a musician like guitarist Gerry Finn, a native of St. John's, Newfoundland, who would ultimately join the Killer Dwarfs when they were already signed to a major label deal in the early nineties, what were the steps required to land himself the gig?

"The steps taken were actually quite simple. I knew I had to become as good a player/musician as I could and then I had to create opportunities for myself. I immersed myself in music, studied privately, played live as often as I could, and later studied music in university for four years. Then I moved to Toronto, the centre of the music business in Canada. Once there, I used my existing connections to get my foot in the door. I had somehow managed to get the gig with the Dwarfs within about a year or so of having landed in Toronto. Yeah, I thought all of it was possible. The notion that I couldn't pull it off never crossed my mind! [laughs]"

When Charlottetown, PEI's Haywire got together, they decided to conquer their local scene before taking on the rest of Canada.

Dave Rashed: "Haywire was conceived in a Tim Hortons in Charlottetown in 1981. It was Marvin, Paul, Scott Roberts, and myself. Our dream was to form a band from three local bands that would eventually be able to do off-island gigs and go on the road to play full-time. So we selected the people that had no commitments or jobs and were free to follow that dream. Our goal was to form a band that would tour Atlantic Canada and eventually Canada. We started to make a great name for ourselves in the club circuit and then we started to focus on writing original songs and looking for a recording contract."

Money is a struggle for any young musician or band. Along with the expenditures that go along with travel, demo recording, rehearsal space, wardrobe, equipment, promotion, etc., there is the matter of living expenses and the necessities of life. The life of a musician can be challenging and can benefit immensely from support of both a moral and financial nature from family and friends.

"My parents really wanted me to go to college after grade twelve," says Haywire's Rashed. "I remember going to the interview with Mr. Paul Seagul, an instructor at Holland College. After the interview process he looked at me and said that I should really pursue my musical interests and when I was ready, come back and the door would always be open at the college. My parents were hoping that after a few years the band would stop and things would get back to normal. Needless to say, they didn't. They really enjoyed all that came with the later success of the band and it was great to share that with them."

"I was very fortunate to have a family that backed me," says Walsh. "When I was fourteen my father paid for my band at the time to go into the studio and cut our first demo. It was so I could gain some real experience, and once I was bitten I was hooked!"

Russ Dwarf had similar backing for the Killer Dwarfs. "My mother supported the band wholeheartedly. She actually put up the money for us to record *Stand Tall* when we got dumped from Attic after our first record."

Friends and family were also supportive of Gerry McGhee's endeavours with Brighton Rock. "Absolutely. I don't think we could have done it if it weren't for my mother, because in those days we were lucky if we were making fifty dollars a week. I have to put my wife in there as well, because she was with me in those days and she was the one working the day job while I was going away for two or three months at a time and coming home with a hundred dollars. So you know, the bank of Mom helped out a lot, the bank of the Wife helped out a lot. They knew that I was driven and that I really, really wanted this and they could see it when they met the other guys that they shared the same ambitions. Unfortunately, I didn't have any education. I quit school when I was sixteen to go on the road, so to me it was all or nothing, but there was definitely good support. My oldest brother, the guy who used to drum music into me, he was the big supporter, and my sisters as well. Yeah, it was supported all around by the family."

For some, the moral support was there but the dues for studying at the School of Hard Knocks were self-paid.

"Moral support, yeah," says Grehan. "I never got any financial support from my family. I wanted to do things on my own, I didn't want any support, and they weren't the kind of family that would throw a lot of money at it. I was kind of out on my own because I went to Fanshawe [College] for a few years and then I moved to Toronto. I had a couple of close friends that were always supportive, but my family, they were happy for me but they weren't the kind of family that shows up at gigs and really supports you. Whereas Johnnie [Dee, lead vocalist for Honeymoon Suite] came from an Italian family and they were so into that — he was the other side of the coin. They were so proud of him and they would help him out and buy him a car and that kind of stuff."

Others were not so lucky and had to find not only the money to fund their new career path but also the intestinal fortitude to stay true to their chosen career path in the face of parental adversity.

"With my family, none at all," claims Lips on the subject of parental support. "Everything that I had to do was on my own. If I had to buy an amplifier or a guitar or strings, anything, I had to find a way to earn the money to be able to do it myself. There was really no support system.

My older brother was probably supportive, I guess, but certainly not my parents. They didn't want a rock star for a son."

For the Canadian metal and hard rock bands of the 1980s, staring down the barrel of a low-paying existence was not enough to derail them from pursuing their rock star dreams. But what constitutes these dreams, or in fact the definition of rock star, seemed to have little to do ultimately with wealth or celebrity. It had much more to do with finding a way to chase the sound that moved them so deeply in their youth and then sharing it with the world. But a band living a pre-Internet existence and not receiving radio play or enjoying major label promotion had to figure out a way to take their show on the road.

the road

As I mentioned before, my buddy Jeff Van Dusseldorp was the keyboardist for a band called Down 'n Dirty, a professional hard rock band on the road, touring across Canada and performing spot-on covers of the day's heavy hits. It was through him that I learned of this mystical place that seemed to exist beyond time and space ... The Road.

A little history here. I had met Jeff when I was in ninth grade at St. Joseph Scollard Hall, the local Catholic high school. After some failed attempts at football, basketball, and uh ... pretty much every sport, I had accepted my fate as a semi-loner who listened to metal. Most of my more athletically-inclined elementary school friends had already graduated to a life of girls and sports, and I was good with that. I actually met my best high school friend, Paul St. Pierre, as a result of a Frosh Week hazing. As we were forced to dress up like clowns, wear makeup, and slow dance as over-amped seniors poured salad dressing over our heads, we staved off the shame and humiliation by whispering about our shared love of Van Halen, Helix, and all things metal. I actually felt that those days of hazing and alienation were part of my larger life story at the time, the beginning of a great triumph of Rock over Jock, so to speak. Then again, our city and school were small enough that those sorts of delineations really kind of faded away within that first awkward year of high school. In North Bay, Jocks, Musos, Nerds, Puck Bunnies, and whatever other group you can think of really kind of bonded over the same sort of things ... finding beer, drinking that beer in a public place, and listening to music.

I had already upgraded from my pawnshop guitar to a brand new Series A guitar loaded with two single coil pickups, a humbucker in the bridge, and most importantly, a Floyd Rose locking tremolo system. The Floyd Rose allowed me to do the dive bomb effects that were a mainstay of any good metal solo (and many bad ones!), and when coupled with the MXR Overdrive that I borrowed from Brock Farquhar (a kid who shared not only my musical interests, but also had a mullet identical to mine), I was a one-man metal machine. I could really only play "Heaven's on Fire" by KISS, but it sounded *right* with this rig.

Jeff found out I played guitar, and since we were both altar boys at the cathedral, a shared love of rock gave us something to talk about during the lengthy sermons. Jeff was a gifted player, and when he would invite me over to his house to demonstrate the sounds he could generate with his Yamaha DX7, I was floored. We would jam out songs by Van Halen and Journey, and as I attempted to rise to his level of proficiency, I could feel my self-esteem rising and my heart racing with each semi-successful attempt at completing a song. We put together our first high school band, complete with a lead singer who was also a star wide receiver on the football team (how's *that* for marketing), kept it Canadian by learning covers of "Born to Be Wild" and "Taking Care of Business," and entered our school's talent show. We didn't win, but none of that mattered. After that show, there was a look in the eyes of girls who had otherwise not really paid that much attention to us (excluding our wide receiver lead singer and ridiculously handsome drummer, Martin Kelly, clearly no relation to me!) that made me think this rock 'n roll thing was a pretty good social move. But far beyond that little perk was the unparalleled *rush* of hearing the music you were performing blasted through a massive PA, and the feeling of having the energy you were giving away thrown right back at you from the crowd. We all felt it, but as the years went on, Jeff took it to the next level.

A year older than me, Jeff began seeking out more experienced musicians (while still playing in our high school band). A player of his calibre and technological savvy was quickly swept up by the hottest players in town. I could not believe when Jeff invited me up to his father's construction company warehouse to showcase his new band for me. The players looked *exactly* like they came out of *Hit Parader* or *Circus* magazines. I mean, I had never seen hair like this before on males in real life (even Helix would have had a hard time matching these glorious barnets!). They bragged about their hair extensions as if they were prized pieces of gear. And the gear they did have was incredible! They had *stacks* of amps, pointy guitars, a double bass drum set ... this was for real. As they rattled off song after song, I was overcome with total jealousy but also excitement. I felt that a door was opening, and I was getting a glimpse of the future. An amazing future where people from North Bay could actually strike out and become rock stars!

When the showcase was done, Jeff popped out from between his stack of keyboards (he was now rocking four keyboards in total, two on each side!) and dropped a bomb on me.

"I'm going on the road!"

At the heart of the heavy metal experience is the live concert performance. Since the dawn of the genre, the in-concert energy exchange between band and audience has provided an adrenaline surge that has proven addictive to both artist and audience. For the Canadian metal and hard rock bands of the eighties and early nineties, the hunt for this adrenaline rush has taken bands on cross-country adventures through Canada's rugged terrain, where life and limb were risked as bands dealt with the challenges of Canadian blizzards, unruly and unwelcoming patrons, and their own quest for the ultimate party!

Glen "Archie" Gamble is a fine example of a musician who has dedicated much of his life to the pursuit of the rock 'n roll dream. He has toured across Canada countless times, performing in venues ranging from the seediest watering holes all the way to some of the country's biggest clubs and arenas. During his time with bands like

Nasty Klass and Vandyl (a band which would see its members depart for the greener career grasses of such acts as Aldo Nova, Lee Aaron, Carl Dixon Band, and Helix), Archie was privy to the rigours of the classic Canadian touring "circuit."

"The touring circuit for us was divided into two sections: Ontario (north and south) and Western Canada (Thunder Bay to Vancouver). Most clubs had live music six or seven nights a week, with either a full week in one place (usually Northern Ontario to out west) or divided weeks (Monday to Wednesday, known as a "Front End" at one club, Thursday to Saturday, or "Back End" at another). I started in 1984 playing occasional weekends and gradually worked my way up to full-time touring by 1987 with Vandyl, and then Nasty Klass."

For more established acts with a recording deal, shows were usually booked by bigger booking agents like S.L. Feldman and Associates and The Agency Group, and they looked to book their bands into bigger concert venues. Smaller clubs in smaller towns were often handled by an agent in each area.

"Thunder Bay had Debbie K. Debbie, Winnipeg had Crazy Steve, Calgary had Pat from Commodore, and in Ontario it was Lapointe-Dubay. Also, the north had a series of small-time agents you would generally have to cut in to play their club. These commissions usually came out of the band's end."

For the clubs and agents who needed to book entertainment, the name of the game was making sure there were as many beer- and liquor-drinking patrons as possible. To achieve this, bands were asked (or more like required) to perform cover songs of the popular hard rock and metal hits of the day (and the days that came before). An enterprising young band composing original music would always look to sneak original compositions into a set that otherwise was jammed with cover versions of hits. From the late seventies on through the dawn of the nineties, there was a considerable amount of venues looking for this type of entertainment.

"That was one of the things that I think definitely set the majority of Canadian bands apart from a lot of American bands," says Daryl Gray of his pre-Helix band, Tracy Kane. "We could tour fifty-two weeks a year and play six or seven nights a week, and sometimes a matinee on Saturday. I think in general it made us stronger performers because you were entertaining people six nights a week. From talking to a lot of our American counterparts of the eighties, they would have a gig a month and they would gear up everything for that one show and they would have a gig a month later. We were definitely playing cover material because when you're sitting in Geraldton, Ontario, they don't want to hear three hours of your originals, no matter how good they are, because they can't go out and buy it and they're not familiar with it. They want to hear stuff they are familiar with and they can dance to. We would always insert two or three of our own songs into the set, strategically placed between two dance songs. If it was a dance-y type song we could just segue right into it. Then people would go 'Hey, who did that last song' and we could say 'Oh, it was ours.'"

In fact, Gray considers his time learning countless cover tunes as playing a pivotal role in the development of his ability to create original material. "We always referred to it as going to university, because every time we had to learn somebody else's chops and how somebody else put a song together, it was analyzed, broken down, and filed away in the memory banks for when we wrote our next song."

In describing the combination of cover songs and originals in the Quebec bar scene, Rick Hughes of Sword saw the combo as complementary.

"I think that one doesn't go without the other, because all the bands that wanted to be a good hard rock band or a good metal band had to play a lot. You wouldn't get hired by the clubs if you only did originals. Sword started as a writing band right from the beginning, but we also had to do the cover thing. For example, we did all the Iron Maiden, the Ozzy, the Dio, which by the way made us really good singers [laughs]. Because we had to imitate those giants, you know? Even if you wanted to be a really original band you still had to imitate others. To play the bar scene we had to do all that stuff. We played a lot of AC/DC, Led Zeppelin, Maiden, Sabbath, and we were writing our own material all at the same time. This lasted for four or five years. The bar would hire you for four or five nights a week. And we had jobs, so here in Quebec the bars go until three in the morning. We would go to bed at four and wake up at six or seven for work."

"Honeymoon Suite started out as a cover band," says Derry Grehan. "It was just, 'Let's get out there because we have to eat.' So we'd have a six-nighter in Timmins and then we'd have another one in Elliot Lake, and then Sudbury. That's what we did, and to do that you have to play covers, so it was like Billy Idol and stuff like that, but that's how you cut your teeth. I also had some original songs. When I first joined Honeymoon Suite I had finally found in Johnnie a guy who could sing. I mean, I had bands and it's really hard to find a singer. When you find that, it's like the light bulb goes off. I knew I had some songs and Johnnie could sing and he could write too, and I thought *Bang, we might have something here*. So we started sneaking 'New Girl Now' and a couple of other songs into the show, and it went from there.

"I wanted Honeymoon Suite to be more than a cover band. The cover thing was just to work. When you would do a six-nighter, you would rehearse during the day if you could, if it's a club that's closed. You would go in there in the afternoon and rehearse. I remember we had a two-week gig up in Sault Ste. Marie at a Holiday Inn and we were working on the first album at that time, and I remember writing 'Stay in the Light' and 'It's Your Heart' up there, rehearsing 'New Girl Now' and 'Burning in Love.' We would go in during the day when the club was closed — it was great. You would have all afternoon, and that's how we'd rehearse."

"Back then you had to play covers," states Russ Dwarf of his pre-Killer Dwarfs band OZ. "You were playing six, seven nights sometimes at the same place, right? So we did sets of all the rock tunes, and we did this one speciality set of Alice Cooper, who is one of my biggest influences. We went everywhere. We went to Newfoundland and back, and it was the crazy days of everybody in a cube van with friends and family. There are a million stories of that comedy! I think I drove to Newfoundland when I was twenty and I didn't even have a driver's licence! And we'd have all the gear in there, and the PA and the lights, and we'd be stuffed in there. But you know, you're young and resilient so you can put up with the comedy, right? You're like pirates [laughs]."

And just like pirates, the reward for a hard day's night involved a blend of liquid and chemical fortification, carnal indulgence, and bar-room brawling.

"Jeez, man, the debauchery that took place in the eighties, what are you gonna say about that?" ponders Lips. "Of course, it was endless, it was crazy, and there are some things that stand out, but you know what? If I start going into that, it becomes a different book [laughs]. That kind of lifestyle just doesn't exist anymore. I mean, once the onset of things like AIDS came, it was over. But previous to that, there were orgies, there were all sorts of things that happened to bands. All that stuff existed, and I was there. I saw some of it, some of it I lived, some of it I didn't bother with because it didn't seem like the right thing to do."

"We got in one real bust-up up in Peterborough one time at a club called Jokers," recounts Brian Vollmer of Helix. "Actually, Jim Carrey opened up for us that night! And at the end of the night Kenny Heague [sound engineer] was walking out with two guitars and a guy tried to trip him, believe it or not, and so I came out and I said, 'Which guy was it?' And Kenny pointed him out and I walked up and just hammered him one. And the next thing I knew there were about fifty people fighting at the back of the room and there was a little riot."

In Vollmer's autobiography, *Gimme an R*, the Helix frontman reels off story after story of encounters with Vietnam vets stalking the band with knives, the band and their fans taking on bikers who ripped off their merchandise, picking up gun-toting hitchhikers who threatened to blow their heads off ... not mention internal dust-ups within their own camp!

"Some of the bands were worse than others, and typically there was a very 'Canadian' sense of politeness around it all. We did try to be as decadent as possible, which isn't exactly easy when you are spending six nights in Geraldton. Granted, Sven Gali always seemed to find trouble, or at least that was their reputation," says Archie Gamble. "Personally, I was too concerned with charming strippers into bed and buying food to worry about partying [laughs]."

Ahh yes, women ... the font of inspiration for countless heavy metal songs, the muse for oh so many album artists and video directors of the day. And to be honest, there was something magnetic about being in a hard rock band in those days, something that could transform a scraggly-haired skinny guitarist into an Adonis. Perhaps there was something in the commonalities between the band's wardrobe and that of the female patrons that helped create the attraction, a hyper-masculinity manifested in the proper application of eyeliner, hair extensions, and spandex? Whatever the reason, the guys may have wanted to kick the band's collective ass, but the girls seemed to understand....

"We partied every night in every town we were in," says Mike Hall of the Killer Dwarfs. "Girls were always around in large numbers, especially in the U.S.A. once we started doing one-nighters and had some MTV exposure. It was not uncommon to see rock babes line up outside the bus after a show. We'd always party and invite the local ladies on board before we moved on to the next town. Some of the special ones might even stay over! I met some absolutely stunning women over the years, way out of my league, of course. But, then again, I played guitar."

"It's the power of being in the spotlight," claims Brian Vollmer of Helix.

Going back to Sven Gali and their reputation as Canada's Bad Boys of Rock, as a young lad in North Bay fascinated with hard rock I too had heard of this Southern Ontario band of reputed ne'er-do-wells and vagabonds. Stories of destroyed hotel rooms, orgies, and rampant drug parties had me and my musician friends shaking with trepidation ... or was it excitement? Regardless, one wonders how much of this was just carefully developed hype and gossip. Or was the truth even stranger and more decadent than the myth?

Well, if it was that bad ... people who have lived it and are now living a decidedly more domesticated lifestyle are probably not going to want to give up too many details. The road makes a man (and woman) do crazy things ... things that you would never do under different circum-stances. But when you factor in complete physical exhaustion due to a lack of sleep (from all-night drives and various stimulants), drinking binges, and twenty-two hours of mind-numbing boredom followed by two hours of rock 'n roll nirvana on stage, things can get crazy.

"I mean, basically, yeah ... I've heard lots of stories and stuff," says Sven Gali's Andy Frank. "I have to say there's only about one or two [sit-uations] that I thought went too far. It was different days, pre-Internet, and we were young and foolish. We've all got young kids. I don't know if I would go into details, but it really was [crazy]. I can't think of other people in Canada that were getting away with some of this stuff — part of it I think was just this frustration of being locked into the crazy, boring club circuit thing. We were young, and everybody seemed to be doing stuff like that, Mötley Crüe and [bands] like that."

In terms of drugs and alcohol, the road is a good place to get both. A young rock band in town to provide the soundtrack for the party could easily find itself on the receiving end of copious amounts of alcohol and drugs. What are the repercussions of such a lifestyle?

"We were never a huge drug band. It was around us but we were mostly drinkers ... Jack Daniels and beer were my faves," claims Hall. "Darrell [Millar, drums] was known to have a few as well. Russ [Graham, vocals] blew his pancreas out pretty early on and as a result couldn't really party that much on the road. A steady diet of McDonalds and Jack Daniels will do that to you. Plus, he was watching his voice, Pavarotti that he is! On occasion somebody would show up and turn us on with whatever they were selling ... but we never really fell into that hole. Who could afford it? [laughs] The bands in the U.S.A. who were really selling lots of records were bona fide cokeheads in the eighties ... smack came later and fucked a few people up. Apparently Nikki Sixx of Mötley Crüe was savvy enough to keep a diary of his flirtation with it, ha-ha, okay, dude! In my opinion, alcohol is the big killer for touring musicians. It's readily available, legal, and socially acceptable. A lot of guys fall into that trap."

It is common to hear about this sort of excess in American bands, so I wondered if sex and drugs played as big a part in the story of Helix, "Canada's Hardest Working Band."

Vollmer: "Well, I don't know ... [sex and drugs] permeates every inch of your life. Like, we did drugs, we had sex, but it wasn't everything. It wasn't something we consciously thought about every day, it was just part of the whole lifestyle. But you know, we did make some wacky decisions. One thing that is not always talked about is sleep deprivation. Not only were we doing drugs, drinking, partying, but also we slept when we were tired, and when we weren't tired we got up ... there was no cycle to our sleep! When Brent Doerner first quit the band, he said 'You know, I slept for two years. It was like I hadn't slept for twenty.' I'm sure there are instances where we had shouting matches or fuck-ups because we'd been drinking or were half hung over, but just as many because we'd only slept two hours the day before!"

When I was writing this, I could have gone pretty deep into the types of debauchery we are talking about here ... but that story has been written countless times. I mean, do you need a psychology degree to know that people in heavy metal bands sometimes liked to drink, do drugs, and have sex? But I did want to know if the sex, drugs, and rock 'n roll life was as prevalent on the Canadian touring scene as it was in say, the Los Angeles scene.

Andy Frank: "Oh, god, yeah. Definitely [laughs]. Certainly I think for Sven Gali, when you talk about life-and-death or near-death experiences, the substances and abuse that we would do to our bodies and stuff, yeah, probably. I mean, nothing that bad, nobody was shooting heroin or anything. That happened other places, it certainly wasn't our thing. There was hard partying, trashing places, couches out the window, that's true [laughs]. I did hear a few stories about us that were like, people getting hurt and stuff, but that certainly never happened. That's way too far. But most of the other stories ... yeah."

Where there is intense partying, there is usually increased volatility. Close quarters and sketchy facilities could lead to all sorts of hijinks.

"One story does stick out," says Doug Weir of Syre. "We were playing Roxanne's in Hull, Quebec. Roxanne's was always a great gig due to its proximity to Ottawa and the fact that the bars were open later in Quebec. There were no rooms at Roxanne's, so we were given rooms at The British, a short drive away. When we arrived, we found that some friends of ours, Steel Lily, were also housed there. This was great fun and we had a few parties on our shared floor. Through the week we had run into a bit of a problem with the hotel. Two rock bands and crews getting ready for their respective shows in the hair band era tend to use a great deal of hot water and blow dryers, and each day we would run out of hot water and blow the fuses of the hotel. This angered the staff, who had to walk down to a dank, dark basement to reset the fuse switches. It also angered us, because we had to be ready for our shows, preferably clean! To piss us off, they tended to stall in turning the power back on.

"The final night of our stay the fuse went, and everyone lost a bit of their composure. One of our guys decided to run through the hotel bar in a hockey mask and his underwear, yelling 'Turn on the power.' [laughs] The locals weren't amused. When Chip Gall [guitar player] and I went to put a few things in our van for the gig, a couple of very drunk older gentlemen came outside and tried to rough us up. They were far too drunk to actually hit us, but they tried. This was followed by a bunch more people coming out of the hotel bar, so Chip and I high-tailed it around to the front of the building. At the same time, our band and crew were coming out the front door, and a bit of a riot ensued. This was at about six o'clock on a Saturday night, so soon most of the town was out on their lawns watching the commotion — it was surreal! After about five minutes the police showed up and separated the two warring factions. Our drummer, Jamie, had forgotten his drum practice pad inside, and the police escorted him back into the hotel, but they quickly ran outside again in a panic, because the hotel was on fire, and ultimately burned to the ground! No one was ever charged, and no one could ever figure out how the fire started!"

One of the interesting aspects of the Canadian touring circuit during the eighties was that there were often two types of entertainment sharing the same venue stage: live rock bands and exotic dancers. The combination brought out some pretty colourful characters, which added to the sense of debauchery, danger, and decrepitude.

"The accommodations were terrible," says Carl Dixon when describing the conditions that Coney Hatch members were living in during their venue residencies on the road. "Every town had a Queen's Hotel or King Edward Hotel, and they were all from the Queen Victoria era, not the Queen Elizabeth era. Red brick, two- or three-storey places where a lot of the local unemployed men lived. Guys living on their pensions who had no homes, they lived in old hotels and drank the days away. That was your company. And there were always strippers in the hotels at that time, too. The strippers went on stage in the afternoon and the bands at night. It was pleasant company, I guess, for a lot of the time, but so often the accommodations were barely acceptable. The worst thing you could encounter was a band house."

Band houses were properties, usually close to the venue, that were purchased by the venue owners to provide accommodation for the bands travelling through town.

"They were always a disaster," continues Dixon, "because they decided no band was worth investing in to keep the place nice. The next band through would just wreck it anyway! It was a continual spiral of downward degradation. The greatest motto I ever heard that explains it all came from a place called the Stone House in Toronto. They actually didn't provide accommodations, but they had a dressing room that was kind of along the same lines of just falling apart, no upkeep. When I asked one of the Greek guys who ran the place, 'Come on, why do you have to let it be like this?' he just looked at us and said: 'All bands ... PIGS.' [laughs]"

Says Doug Weir, "Our accoms were hit and miss, but in most cases we didn't really care. A lot of partying went on in those days and you'd pretty much fall into a bale of hay if it was close at hand. We usually stayed in the hotels where we played, or in a band house. We were staying in a band house in Fredericton, New Brunswick ... great place, except it got broken into while we were playing and we lost a chunk of change!"

Derry Grehan concurs. "It was real bare-bones, you're living in hotels, sharing rooms, and there are rummies on the same floor, but you're happy to be there. As long as you've got some cold beer and you're playing at night, that's good enough when you're twenty-one or twenty-two years old, right?"

Brian Vollmer explains how Helix survived on some of those long winter nights. "Well, in the early days of the band when we were on the circuit, there were terrible rooms. I don't even know how they could get approved by whoever from the city approves rooms [laughs]. Because a lot of them didn't have any heat, you froze in them. A lot of them didn't have enough bathrooms. You had to use the bathroom down the hall, which you know, the wino/junkie/whoever used. It wasn't until later on that we actually started to get half-decent rooms and even when we toured the United States the first time, we were down there on such a shoestring budget that we got like, they were like holes. I remember one time we played in Rochester, New York, and it was one of the coldest days in Rochester history and Bill Seip [Helix's manager] had got us these cheap, cheap, cheap rooms and they had no heat in them. And me and Paul [Hackman, guitarist] were in one room, and I remember we pulled all the blankets in one bed, we put our boots on, about six sweaters, coats, hats, gloves, everything, and we got into bed. When we woke up in the morning it was like *Planes, Trains and Automobiles*, we were face to face in a bear hug [laughs]."

Under these less than luxurious circumstances, a stiff upper lip and a good sense of humour were survival requirements, according to Killer Dwarfs frontman Russ "Dwarf" Graham. "Our motto was you've gotta laugh or you're gonna cry, because it's tough out there, you know? Here's your eleven bucks for the week, I got my loaf of bread and some Cup-a-Soup. One day Darrell [drummer] comes in when we were playing a gig and he got a Snack Pack from Kentucky Fried Chicken and we were like 'Where the hell did you get that?' Everybody was freaking out, and he was like, 'Uh, I pawned the hotel vacuum cleaner.' [laughs] I mean, you could not make this shit up! But we loved music and we were young. When you're that young you can take anything, you're just pounding it out."

Heavy metal and hard rock performances are often about much more than music. The music lends itself to a flashy presentation, and many of the more successful bands of the genre picked up on the importance of the visual element of putting on a good show, even if it was on a budget in the early days.

Victor Langen: "Back when Kick Axe started playing live, the Alberta hotel bars were huge 700-seaters. Every night was a concert vibe, and we used all the tricks ... fog, dry ice, pyro, follow spotlights, and strobes. Live music was a booming business for Alberta hotels in the late seventies, and we were putting on shows in Calgary, Edmonton, Medicine Hat, Red Deer, Lethbridge, etc. Of course, our manager and agents made more money than we did."

When hair metal started taking hold in the mid to late eighties, the visual aspects of touring took on even greater importance.

"The look was *everything*," states Gamble, "as was the show. If you didn't have a good 8 x 10 promo photo, with the right clothes and hair, you wouldn't even be considered. Once you got in, you had to back it up with the right PA, lights, and choreography. Bottom line was, if you sucked, you didn't eat. I was fortunate enough to be in good bands that worked as much as we wanted to. Fifty weeks a year we chose to work, with one week off in the summer and one week off at Christmas. I literally lived in hotels and taverns, and I wouldn't trade it for the world. It makes you a better musician, and I wish younger musicians today had as much opportunity to play live as we did."

Killer Dwarfs were well known for their high-energy performances. Russ Dwarf explains the genesis of their live approach. "We ended up with a manager, Rob Connelly. He was involved with Lee Aaron and a whole bunch of other things. Dave Kirby was also involved with that early stage of our career, and I guess he had a bunch of tribute acts and stuff. At one point we were the low people on the totem pole of his roster. Anywhere we went we were always the underdogs and we weren't treated that great. You know, we would get the scrapings of everything. One day we went into the office and they had this great idea: let's change the name [at this point the band was working under the name Sphynx], because Bryce, Ange, and me are all around 5'4", the same height, right? So Kirby and Connelly came up with this idea to call the band the Killer Dwarfs, and of course we were like, 'What the fuck are you talking about? This is ridiculous.' But we bought into it. So we went with that, and we always had a show business kind of thing, I guess from probably growing up loving KISS and Trooper. Our motto was you get the $350 show for two bucks. At that point of the early Dwarfs, we would dress like cavemen and stuff, we grew beards and I wore a loincloth and we used to swing out over the audience. We had a whole bunch of antics. I chopped up teddy bears and wore a Godzilla head. It was crazy, it was like a circus."

Canada is a *bitch* of a country to tour across. The vast geography and great distances between major cities make for very challenging touring conditions. Long drives under gruelling internal and external conditions can do one of two things: kill you or make you stronger.

Gerry McGhee, Brighton Rock: "Well, they always tried to route it so that you were basically making a sweep across the country. One of the things with Brighton Rock is we pretty well did more gigs than anybody else. We would go twenty-one days without a day off. We would literally do no less than six nights a week, and sometimes that is hard when there is such a big gap between cities. I remember we were on a West Coast tour and the album was just about to come out. We flew back from Calgary, did the 'We Came to Rock video,' flew back out the next day, then drove to Vancouver to do a show the following night. So there was a lot of time spent on the road. When we came home we got maybe a day or two days and then we were back out again, because for every album we basically toured for a year and a half."

Carl Dixon, Coney Hatch: "We spent lots of hours in vans. I remember our first time going up to northern Quebec. We borrowed Steve Shelski's [guitar] mom's station wagon [laughs]. The crew had the van for the equipment but we had to get ourselves, the players, there. We had a radiator leak when we were on the way home, so we decided to pull over by a ditch because it was overheating, and somebody decided the water from the ditch would be good to put in the radiator. The ditch water had who-knows-what in it, and by the time we got it home his mom's engine was seized up from the crap water in the radiator!"

Russ Dwarf, Killer Dwarfs: "There was never any place too far [laughs]. Our manager would say "It's only *this* far on the map!" Some of the drives were hell, utter hell! Everybody would be pissing in milk jugs because you've just got to get to the gig, right? You've gotta do fourteen-hour drives in a couple of vans or a cube van and a truck."

Doug Weir, Syre: "We always marvelled at our agent's ability to put us on tours which, when drawn on a map, resembled the Star of David. Syre toured about fifty weeks a year, so to us it didn't really matter, we were already 'out there.' We started touring in an old Bell Canada van that our drummer owned and was kind enough to let us use. We used to pop the cover off the engine inside to hold the carburetor open to start it. We also had a number of reworked school buses. Our paint jobs became kind of a hard rock Partridge Family motif. When we started to use motor homes and real buses it was like heaven."

Harry Hess, Harem Scarem: "It was ridiculous. I remember even thinking about our agent, 'Does this guy even own a map? Does he know what he's doing to us?' I remember being in frigging Calgary and going to do two nights in Vancouver, and then coming back somewhere in the middle. And we're like 'Why wouldn't we do that first and then fly back?' But you know, looking back you realize the agent is at the mercy of whatever club can book you on that date, and you'd have to take the dates and be happy about them for the most part. But even then I remember thinking *There's gotta be a better way* [laughs]."

Gerry McGhee, Brighton Rock: "We were playing in Quebec in the winter with Honeymoon Suite when our first record came out. I think you could see Labrador from where we were, that's how far north it was. By this point, Honeymoon Suite had been rolling, I think their album was approaching double platinum at the time. It was their first headlining tour and we were the opening act. They had this gorgeous big Eagle tour bus, and we had a Cadillac Coupe De Ville that we borrowed from Chris Gauthier, who we rented our lighting system from. We did the entire tour with the five of us in this Coupe De Ville and we actually put a towel with our logo on it on the front grille to stop it from freezing. While Honeymoon Suite were riding around in their tour bus with bunks and stereos and coolers, there were five of us and a cooler driving around in the Cadillac and our crew in a truck. It was pretty well that way our whole career. Lucky for us we finally got to the point where we got our own bus [laughs]."

Rob Urbinati, Sacrifice: "You don't realize how big this country is until you drive from the Atlantic to the Pacific. We loved touring Canada, even though we were sleeping on our Marshalls in the back of a van, freezing, listening to the same cassette tapes over and over, driving an average of nine or ten hours between shows. First we started playing a few shows in Quebec and Ontario, then we went all-out and started doing nationwide tours. Some of my best memories were touring Canada with Razor. It felt like we were both carrying the flag everywhere we went."

Nick Walsh, Slik Toxik: "I remember totally slumming it. Very rarely did we get a chance to even stay overnight in the places we played in the early days. It was brutal. We would rent a cube truck and put not just our gear in the back, but also our jam space furniture to create the best makeshift tour bus money could buy [laughs]. There are no windows or ventilation in the back of a cube, so we took a laundry dryer tube, hooked it up to the front window and sent it back so we could have some fresh air. Sleeping on Marshall 4X12 guitar cabinets wasn't the most comfortable, though!"

Touring through Canada's rugged terrain can be challenging enough in the best of weather. But taking on the Trans-Canada Highway in winter is always a wild-card type of situation. You never know what Mother Nature is going to throw at you, and you have to be prepared to deal with it. The only way to truly understand what this kind of lifestyle is like is to experience it yourself. These first-hand accounts from the artists may be the closest an outsider can get ... or would want to get!

Derry Grehan, Honeymoon Suite: "Touring Canada, you've got to leave a lot of time, especially in fucking wintertime. What you think is a four-hour drive turns into an eight-hour drive in the winter. It's brutal, and it can also be deadly, driving Sault Ste. Marie over to Winnipeg through that Trans-Canada Highway up over Lake Superior. It's treacherous. I almost got killed a couple of times sliding off the road with those trucks whizzing by. I'm lucky I'm still alive. That's the thing about Canada, it's a massive country, but there are only a few cities and they are really far apart."

Brian Vollmer, Helix: "Oh, it was so cold and sometimes we didn't sleep half the night. In the early, early days of the band we used to come home after the gig at Kapuskasing, we'd have to ride in the back of the goddamn truck and you couldn't tell the driver when you had to stop and take a piss. You'd be banging and hollering away and they couldn't hear you up front. It was whenever they decided to stop. So enter the pee bottle. But there'd be gear falling down around our heads and it'd be freezing fucking cold back there [laughs]."

Mike Hall, Killer Dwarfs: "I remember meeting black ice on my first tour with the Killer Dwarfs. I joined the band in the summer of 1984. The first record was out and the band had already toured coast to coast in Canada once. Even before I was in the band, Russ and I were very close friends and were writing songs and hanging out. When the guitar player quit, I was in between semesters at Berklee and I agreed to help them find a new guy. I ended up joining the band instead.

"I went out on my first national tour in late fall 1984. We played clubs, front ends and back ends, full weeks and some one-nighters. We ground it out in Ontario through Barrie, Sault Ste. Marie, Sudbury, Hearst, Wawa, Cochrane, etc. Once we hit Winnipeg it was a full week at the Zoo, a popular rock bar. Then a front end in Regina, finally getting to Alberta where we did full weeks in Edmonton and Calgary followed by a split week in Red Deer and Lethbridge. Most of the bars were packed, we did good business and sold lots of beer. I remember it being really fucking cold and snowy already in the west, overcast, freezing, grey days. We were pulling down a whopping $150 each a week and eating at 7-11. Three hotdogs for ninety-nine cents — nice. In those days we were travelling in a Dodge camper. We had a three-man crew who drove a five-ton truck with backline and our massive rental PA and light show, courtesy of RAM Audio.

"Now we were faced with making it through the Rockies to Vancouver. I think we had a date booked in Kamloops on the way. It was snowing when we left Alberta. I was crashed out in the back of the camper. Russ was at the wheel. I woke up somewhere in the mountains to nervous laughter from the front. As I made my way up I realized something was very wrong. The camper was sliding sideways down a steep embankment. Russ was laughing that semi-hysterical 'oh man we are *fucked*' laugh and was trying to maintain control. Darrell was riding shotgun, white as a ghost, eyes like saucers … and a beer between his legs. The conversation went something like this:

Mike [half asleep]: 'Hey what the fuck's happening, man?'

Darrell: 'Dude, we're sliding all over … it's black ice!'

Mike [half asleep, but now scared]: 'Well, stop it, man, you're freaking me out!'

Russ: 'Fuuuuuuuck!'

Death lay on both sides of this lonely, dark, ice-covered mountain road. Somehow, Russ brought the camper to a halt at the bottom of the hill. He saved our hides for sure. We sat there for a minute. Then we just shrugged it off and kept going. Lesson one, no more fall-winter touring … ever. From then on, winter was a time for writing tunes and drinking beer."

Harry Hess, Harem Scarem: "We used to drive through the mountains in a frigging Winnebago or a van in a snowstorm. You'd look down and the cliffs are like forty, fifty feet down. There are no guardrails. Like, how many bands risked their lives to play in a shit club for fifty bucks? It's insane."

Michel "Away" Langevin, Voivod: "When Voivod moved to Montreal, we had to go and play shows up north either to our hometown or other parts of Quebec, and most of the places we went you had like a couple of hours through the woods in the snow and it's always pretty scary. Nowadays, it's better because they have larger highways to go through the woods, but back then it was this smaller road where you would cross paths with huge trucks filled with wood and all that, so it was pretty scary at times for sure. We tend to tour in tour buses nowadays because touring in a van is always kind of scary [laughs]."

The whole point of this touring was to bring the music to the people, and the hope was that with each successive return to a market, more people would show up at the concerts based on the band's previous performance. This grassroots groundswell would in turn give local radio programmers a reason to add the artists to their playlist, which would then encourage fans to buy the band's music. Once the band was selling records, they could then hope to garner larger guarantees from the concert venues, and the increase in crowds would then generate an increase in merchandise sales.

Harry Hess shares his views on the measurable benefits of hitting the road, "We really did see an increase in fan base due to touring. At the time the only thing you could do to promote your music aside from touring was get on MuchMusic, get on the radio, and do as much print media and other media stuff as you possibly could. So touring was the way to get out in front of people. Doing opening gigs was a way of getting in front of somebody else's crowd to hopefully win people over so they would become your fans. On our first record and then our second record we could do small clubs on our own because we had a couple of singles that charted at radio. We had a video in rotation and that could get you on an opening slot to go across the country and do bigger venues. On our second record, a big deal for us was opening for April Wine across the country, because it was all basically hockey arenas and stuff like that. So that was great for us and I can only imagine that was helping build our fan base because we were getting out in front of a lot of people who didn't know who we were. You would roll into town, do the local radio, which would usually be sponsoring the show, and you would get a lot of airtime just because you were there. Everybody in our camp, from the label, to the management, to the agent, said that once you're in town you can do the local print media, the radio stations, the record store signings, meet-and-greets before and after the show, and just build on that."

"We quickly grew our audience in most places we played. Most of our audience was female, and with a large female audience, the boys started to come out too," adds Doug Weir of Syre.

"When the looks matched the hooks, the girls would come to the shows, and the boys would follow and end up buying the merch," Carl Dixon affirms.

"Apparently we were a pretty boy band and we didn't even know it. Tons of girls used to show up and then what we learned later was guys would say, 'Well, where the girls are is where I'm going.' We played a very tough kind of music. Not heavy metal, but hard and heavy kind of rock 'n roll, pretty loud and aggressive. The girls would tolerate it because they liked the way we looked and the way we dressed, the tight trousers, etc., and the guys just found the heaviness appealing. There was an age difference, of course, between our bar clientele, which was young males and females over the age of what would have been nineteen at that point, and the people who bought our albums, who were mostly fourteen-to-eighteen-year-old black T-shirt-wearing kind of high school guys. Girls didn't buy our albums so much, but I know that we had a fanatical following among the young guys because we were lumped in at that time with the heavy metal bands like Judas Priest and Iron Maiden. We toured with both bands. So that would be the way the audience built up."

When you hear about bands like Harem Scarem and Coney Hatch comparing their early touring experiences with their later rise to hockey arenas, it raises a question: How do you make that leap? What is the deciding factor that pulls a band from relative bar band obscurity to playing in large concert venues with major artists?

It all goes back to the ultimate goal, the elusive brass ring ... the signing of a recording contract.

BIG F**KIN' DEAL
(LIFE IN THE BIG LEAGUES)

Imagine a business deal that is designed as follows: you create a product, one that is unique and has the potential to generate hundreds of thousands of dollars. The commercial viability of your product is then recognized by people who have generated *millions* of dollars in manufacturing, packaging, and marketing similar products. They offer you the means to manufacture and replicate your product. They will take your product to market, promote it, and if all goes well, ensure that they can be involved in the development of this idea. In exchange for their services and investment, they are going to take between 84 and 88 percent of the profits and leave you with 12 to 16 percent. Also, they are going to try to collect a good chunk of the royalties from the intellectual properties that are the core of that product. They are also going to want the exclusive rights to your next batch of products. And of course, they are going to decide how much money they will invest in these products (without necessarily consulting you) and then recoup that money out of *your* 12–16 percent. This will make it almost impossible to earn anything from the sales of your product. All of this will be written into a document (let's call it a contract) that is roughly the size of the Bible, written in legalese that requires a good eight years of university to suss out, but which generally states that they will own the rights to exploit your product "in perpetuity" (*forever*) for all territories in the "known universe." Sounds a little lopsided, right? Who in their right mind would go for a deal like that?

Ask that of a band that has been grinding it out in the bars, hotels, and taverns that litter the Trans-Canada Highway and the answer might surprise you. When an artist is bitten by the music bug, there is an allure and romance attached to securing a recording contract that defies standard logic. After years of performing the music of other people in some pretty scary conditions for very little money, you start to wonder what it must be like to *be* the artists whose songs you are covering. Record labels spent a lot of money in the eighties making sure that their artists looked like they had all the money in the world at their disposal ... flashy clothes, massive lighting and stage rigs, more pyro than the fires of hell. It sure seemed a lot more glamorous to be on *that* side of the business than in the bars and clubs. And with so many bands aching for that one-in-a-million shot at the opportunity to get signed and break through commercially to millions of fans, it must have been pretty easy to push aside conventional business wisdom for the validation and thrill of getting to record *your* music in a fancy studio, and hopefully land on a major tour that would eventually lead to your own headlining status.

In my daydreaming youth, I would often retreat to my bedroom, pull out some vinyl, and stare at the artwork. The record company logos that emblazoned the backs of the sleeves represented something incredibly exotic, almost otherworldly. I imagined being signed to those labels as being invited into a special club, and each label had its own flavour and appeal. Would I be a part of WEA's (Warner/Elektra/Atlantic) slick roster of AOR-friendly hard rock *à la* Honeymoon Suite, Brighton Rock, or Harem Scarem? Would I be uncorking a bottle of champagne at Hollywood and Vine in Los Angeles at the famed Capitol Records building and seeing my band's poster on the walls alongside Helix? Or would I be keeping it fully Canuck and releasing albums on Attic Records, vying for president Al Mair's attention with Lee Aaron and Anvil? It all seemed ultra-glamorous.

Yeah, man ... I wanted to get *signed*. It didn't really matter to what, or to whom, but just give me a record with my name on it and a big label logo on the back! Did other artists feel that way? Or was it just a means to an end?

"I think it's just part of the natural progression of your career," says Russ Graham. "Back in the days before the Internet you needed to have an international record deal to get your records into all these countries. It wasn't like you could make a record in your living room in your underwear, and with one click you're on iTunes."

"In 1985, after extensive touring and paying our dues in the clubs, we knew that landing a recording contract was the next step for the band's future," says Haywire keyboardist David Rashed. "We thought that was the next logical step to make a career in the music industry. I felt that signing a deal was like entering a partnership where we both had the same goals ... if one party was successful then both were successful."

"It was all about funding!" says Darby Mills of Headpins. "That was how it was done at the time. Recording contracts got you access to that, hopefully. There was no information highway back then, and the networking was very much under the control of the labels."

Helix's Daryl Gray: "We wanted to get records out to people, we wanted to play the big venues. I wanted to play Madison Square Garden and Nassau Coliseum, these big hockey sheds you saw the big bands going into. I wanted to play in front of a lot of people, playing original material."

For Harem Scarem's Harry Hess, getting signed was a step up the music business ladder. "Getting a record deal did put us in another category, at least in our own minds [laughs]. Either you were a touring bar band doing covers and you had a few originals, or you were a recording act, you know? When you're a recording act signed to a reputable label, it does change things because you can demand more money and get it. We could get more gigs. Our agent at the time, S.L. Feldman, wouldn't book you unless you were a recording act, so many things changed for us once we had that label. Once you could say, 'Yeah, we are signed to Warner,' many things changed for Harem Scarem for the better."

Was signing that deal also a personal justification for your artistic endeavours? A status symbol in the scene from whence you came?

"For sure," confirms Coney Hatch's Carl Dixon. "It's a measure of accomplishment that somebody thinks you're worthy and they're going to make money off you, so they have given you this platform. I didn't recognize it as such at that time, but on a subconscious level you understand. 'Wow, I'm pissing with the big dogs now.' [laughs] There's *me* and The Beatles in the same record store! And they're in the Bs and we're in the Cs, oh my god we're almost right next to them! Anthem Records had a cool cachet at that time because they had Rush and Max Webster as part of their roster, so we thought 'Oh man, this is the coolest.' A record deal provides a platform to be heard. Otherwise you're just barking your songs out into the night on a dark stage in a bar and they're lost the moment the song is done. A record means you have created something that people have invested in and they are giving it a chance to be heard by the world after that."

"Absolutely, absolutely," affirms Anvil's Lips. "There's no doubt about it. We were one of the first. Us and Coney Hatch were really the only signings at that time. It was a very rare thing, and we were probably the two hardest-working bands during that period. There were other bands like the Killer Dwarfs, who were also managed by Bruce Wilson, who came behind us. Originally they were signed to Attic as well."

A few years later, Gerry McGhee and Brighton Rock would find themselves signing their own record deal. "In those days everybody wanted to sign to a big label. That really meant you had a shot at a global career. Although it's great to make it here in Canada, bands like The Tragically Hip are rare, few, and far between."

"Of course, but it was also a means to an end somewhat," says Slik Toxik's Nick Walsh. "I was hoping to have people backing up my creative talents with moral and monetary support. People seem to think that when you get signed, you've made it. In my book, it's more like being accepted to a well-to-do college or university. Once that happens, the hard work begins if you want to succeed."

Hess also saw signing a record deal for Harem Scarem as an inevitable step in reaching a broader audience. "There was no other way that we saw to get to what would be considered a large mainstream audience around the world. When we did our deal with Warner Music Canada, we did a world deal. I mean, we never actually understood what that meant until years later. We were signed in Canada, and then it was up to each individual Warner territory in the world whether or not they decided to release our record. For better or for worse, a lot of territories really liked us and some didn't want anything to do with us."

For Honeymoon Suite's Derry Grehan, whose band would aptly name their second major label release *The Big Prize*, a record deal offered an escape from the dank surroundings of the bar scene and a crack at the world's biggest music market, the United States of America. What did he think would happen when he signed a deal?

"We thought we would get to make a record and get out of the bars. We wanted to make a record, get on the radio, and hopefully get some support tours with major acts and play bigger venues. We had the bonus of signing in the States, so we were going from a six-nighter in Elliot Lake, Ontario, to being on a big bus and touring the States a few months later. I was on top of the world going through America, even as an opening act for bands like Heart, ZZ Top, Journey, and .38 Special. It was so amazing."

Killer Dwarfs also had their eyes on south-of-the-border success. For the Dwarfs, signing a record deal with a U.S. label meant bigger production budgets and also a bigger cash advance. An advance is money against recoupable royalties that a band uses to buy copious amounts of cocaine, mansions, expensive sports cars … oh wait. It might be a little more along the lines of actually affording three square meals a day and some new cowboy boots. But you get the idea.

Russ Graham: "We knew we had to get to the US of A, that was where it was happening, right? Getting our music out there was one of our major goals. We signed with Epic out of New York, and it was a dream come true, it was insane. All of a sudden things totally did a 180 for us … we got the big deal, and that's why we called our first album for Epic *Big Deal*. We could actually eat and buy some clothes. We were able to move production-wise as far as our records went. That was amazing — we went from doing a record for, like, ten grand to a budget of 200,000 dollars!"

Harry Hess points out the necessity of record label support back when Harem Scarem signed with Warner. "Getting signed was an acceptance into that world, you would figure. 'Now I have a shot at getting on the radio, now I'm going to make a video.' All of those things were a giant deal back them because without them you were kind of dead in the water — you couldn't compete. You couldn't just turn on your laptop and start recording like you can today. There was a monetary incentive to get signed to a major label. Not because we would be instantly rich, which was very far from the truth, but because you have resources that would enable you to record, make videos, and do all the things necessary to become successful."

Along with the major labels of the day (Warner, Capitol/EMI, Polygram, MCA, RCA, Epic, Columbia, etc.), independent labels helped spread the Canadian heavy metal gospel. Attic Records, founded in 1974 by Al Mair and Tom Williams, was responsible for bringing acts like Lee Aaron, Anvil, Haywire, and Razor to the market, as well as putting out early records by Killer Dwarfs and Triumph.

The Killer Dwarfs and Anvil actually self-financed their first recordings, which then attracted the attention of Attic Records, which ended up licensing the right to exploit and distribute the master recordings.

"We did it all on our own in the sense that we paid for our first recording," says Lips. "It wasn't like we got discovered and somebody paid for it. We blocked out times at a studio in Oshawa called Quest Studios, from Paul La Chapelle who owns the place — a very, very good guy and a very, very fair businessman who gave us a great deal on studio time. We recorded our first album there with no producer, just ourselves. Our manager, Bruce Wilson, invited the guys from Attic Records down to see us play at The Gasworks in Toronto, and we got the deal."

Montreal's Aquarius Records was founded in 1969 by Terry Flood, Bob Lemm, Dan and Jack Lazare, and Donald Tarlton, more famously known as Donald K. Donald, one of Canada's biggest concert and event promoters. Aquarius is most famous as the label that brought classic rockers April Wine and power-pop heartthrob Corey Hart to international acclaim. The label also released proto-hard rock albums by Montreal's Teaze (a band that made little headway in North America but can lay legitimate claim to the title of "Big in Japan"), Rick Hughes' Sword and Saints & Sinners projects, and later albums by bands like Helix and Deep Purple.

Just like Anvil, Sword also followed their entrepreneurial muse and hit the studio before a deal was secured. "When we started to write our own material, we only got six or seven songs ready, then we said 'Let's go into a studio in Montreal and start to record.' We very carefully edited and picked the songs. When you play 'Number of the Beast,' 'Bark at the Moon,' or 'Holy Diver' in a live set and then put an original song in that nobody has ever heard before, it kind of passes by, you know? But when you're in the studio doing an album, it's another thing. You put them under the microscope. We listened and thought *Wow, what the hell, this is good!* So in the studio, the guy who was producing the demo made some calls and went to the record companies. We didn't even have time to finish the seven-song pre-production demo to present to record companies because a contract was offered to us while we were in the studio, from Aquarius Records."

Solid Gold Records was co-founded by Steve Propas and Neil Dixon and had great success with classic rock radio staples Chilliwack and two of Canada's pioneering female-fronted hard rock acts, Toronto (led by vocalist Anne "Holly" Woods and guitarist Sharon Alton) and Headpins.

Other indie labels putting out Canadian hard rock and metal product at the time were Maze Records (home of Killer Dwarfs' classic *Stand Tall* album), Fringe Product (handling thrash acts like Razor, Slaughter, and Sacrifice), and Ready Records (home to Toronto's hard-rockin' hometown heroes Santers and new wave acts like The Spoons and Blue Peter).

These companies may not have had the corporate reach or infrastructure of their major label contemporaries, but they would often align with a major for use of their distribution, pressing, and marketing and promotional services. Because these "indies" felt less pressure to adhere to a corporate bottom line, they had more manoeuvrability in terms of the acts they could sign, acts that might not have had a chance to get a record released. There is a certain cachet about being with an independent label, an underground vibe that resonates with disenfranchised youth looking for something unique, something that is their own. Having said that, there definitely appeared to be a hierarchy amongst bands that had a lot to do with the types of deals they signed. The major coup seemed to be signing directly to the U.S. The second-best scenario would be a domestic major label signing with releases in other territories. The bronze prize would go to those with an independent deal with some sort of distribution pipeline.

To the average fan, the details as to who pays for, markets, and distributes the albums of their favourite bands probably doesn't matter one iota. However, when I think back to the days of the 12.375-square-inch cardboard album sleeve and extensive liner notes, I realize that this information did matter to me, and in fact informed my own dreams. I romanticized those record company logos and visualized them as some sort of gateway to the life I desperately wanted to lead. And you could sometimes tell just by looking at the album cover which bands had a major label deal and which bands had an indie deal. There was a slickness inherent in the packaging of Coney Hatch's *Outta Hand* and Helix's *Wild in the Streets* that seemed just slightly above the visual production value of a similar album by, say, Vancouver "muscle rock" act Thor's *Keep the Dogs Away* or Razor's *Armed and Dangerous*. Then again, you could make an argument that the underground vibe of the indie artwork added credibility to those acts, a street-level approach that was more in line with the true intent of what metal and hard rock were supposed to stand for.

Major label or independent, one thing common in both types of deals was the binding legal document that laid out their terms, the much-coveted and often misunderstood contract. Historically, artists are notoriously bad businesspeople. I mean, once you have experienced the rush of creating and performing your own music, how can you possibly want to be concerned with such petty details as royalties, music publishing, tour support, etc.? This is what managers and lawyers are for, right? Right?

So, did our hard rock and heavy metal heroes understand the legal language inherent in their record deals? Were the legalities even a concern for them? Not for Russ Dwarf.

"Lord, no, the thing was like 186 pages! Obviously, hindsight is 20/20. If you could go back in time it would be great. Our manager's brother was a lawyer, and we had our own lawyers and everything. So it's someone else's business, right? My job was to create music and do the shows."

How about Lips from Anvil?

"Obviously not. I signed the thing, and it was a foolish thing to have done. Maybe it could have been negotiated, but it's interesting, we were trying to negotiate so we asked our lawyer at the time, 'Is there anything we can do to make this better?' and he said 'I highly doubt it.' It was like, take it or leave it. So we just went with it. I don't even know if we could have foretold what was to be. Some of the stuff in the deal was standard, some of the stuff is of its day and age. Now, in this day and age, those kinds of contracts just do not exist. You don't do licensing deals forever.

Our deal was a licensing deal, and we basically signed our first three albums away forever. To this day I don't own those."

"Our music lawyer made us aware that it was a one-sided deal, but since it was the only deal that we had in front of us, we decided to take it and see if we could make it work," says Haywire's Rashed.

Sometimes, even when a band was given sound legal counsel, the fear that they might be missing their one and only shot could blind them from making a sound legal decision. Brighton Rock's Gerry McGhee breaks down his deal with Brighton Rock as follows:

"We had a manager who took care of it, and after we signed a management contract he suggested we get a lawyer. And he referred to it as putting the cart before the horse, and that it was a bad deal all the way around. We were signed to a production company, and that company was responsible for recording Brighton Rock records and the production company would then license the record to Warner Music. The production agreement, which was absolutely asinine, commissioned the videos and the albums, so if Warner gave us $100,000 to record an album, they would get a percentage of that. And that money is completely recoupable, that's not money earned, that's an advance. So that $15,000 or $20,000 taken as a commission could be the difference between making our third album, *Love Machine*, or making Bon Jovi's *Slippery When Wet*. You should never take away money from the production of the record. And they did the same thing with videos. After we fired them all, after I took control, it was the first time the guys were actually walking around with cash, you know, looking at buying houses, new cars. And that was on the downswing of the band. I was seen as the troublemaker in the beginning because I had a brother-in-law who was a chartered accountant. He went through the contracts left, right, and centre and said that these were bad, bad, bad deals and we should not sign these. The guys kind of felt that I was going to rock the boat because at the time our manager was looked at like the new Brian Epstein — everybody loved him, he was successful. So I basically bit my tongue and signed the deal so that we could do the record in the hope that after the initial three to five records were done, we would be in a position where we could start to actually make money. But it never got that far."

Carl Dixon of Coney Hatch fared slightly better thanks to his diligence in informing himself.

"I was aware, but I made a point of it. I was actually the least willing to sign the deal, to tell you the truth. I had to be convinced and coerced and I was getting pressure: 'C'mon, stop dragging this out, what's wrong?' We had a very good lawyer who is still our friend today, advising us we shouldn't sign the deal. All the while Anthem was insisting 'C'mon, time's wasting, let's get on this,' which is a tactic in itself, how you push young guys and try to capitalize on their excitement and the stars in their eyes, and they sign any damn thing. Plus I was getting some unexpected caution from [producer] Kim Mitchell's wife, who knew the guy that ran Anthem Records. She was cautioning me, 'Carl, he doesn't really care that much. His focus is more on real estate now and getting into movies, I don't think this is right for you, I would really think about this.' So I really thought about it [laughs]. Ultimately, they did make some concessions in the record deal and I was aware of the impact those would have. It meant that we would start making publishing money at least from the very first record sold, rather than [with] so many Canadian bands who signed deals where they never saw a penny for their records, either publishing or mechanicals. So I'm glad I held out for that reason. I really paid attention and read the contracts myself and listened to what our lawyer was telling us, whereas I don't think everybody else in the band was so quite so diligent in that regard."

It is easy to paint the record labels as villains in these scenarios, but one could also make the argument that this is simply a case of supply and demand. With so many bands willing to do anything for a shot at bringing their music to the masses in the hopes of living the rock 'n roll dream, were the labels not somehow obliged by the rules of the jungle that is the free enterprise market to get the most they could from the artists for the least amount of investment?

Moral and ethical issues aside, these artists wanted record deals, and the labels were offering 'em. But how did these bands attract the interest of the artist and repertoire (A&R) executives at these companies? What was the difference between bands that would see some garnering hundreds of thousands of dollars in label investment while others were rejected and left to fend for themselves? How did these bands get signed?

Getting signed was a process that involved getting the attention of A&R executives and then convincing them that your band was going to be a money-maker. A band had to have a magical combination of great songs, a marketable look, and the oft-cited but rarely defined "X" factor, that element that would convince an A&R rep to put his neck and his job on the line and commit to the vast amount of development dollars it would take to push an artist into the marketplace.

For Helix, it was the combination of the aforementioned elements and a tireless work ethic that sealed the deal. The band had already proven itself as a viable commercial entity by selling over 20,000 units of its two independent albums, *Breaking Loose* and *White Lace and Black Leather*. They also had managed to attract serious radio attention south of the border, largely thanks to the support of San Antonio radio jockey and metal impressario Joe Anthony, who had previously championed Canuck acts like Rush and Moxy.

"We would showcase for several labels before we were finally signed, and showcased for Capitol five or six times," says Vollmer. "Capitol finally decided to sign us at The Gasworks in Toronto. Dean Cameron, who was the head of A&R at the time, had left after our second set but sneaked back in the rear door to watch us without us knowing. Brent's amp had blown up at the end of the second set, and without batting an eye, he set up his little practice amp and mic'ed it. We then proceeded to take the stage and rock out like nothing was the matter. Dean told us that was what clinched the deal for us. They knew we would work our balls off for them if they gave us a chance."

Voivod's recording contract with Metal Blade records came as a result of the "tape trading" scene of the eighties, a precursor to today's Internet file sharing. Fans of the thrash genre would become pen pals through international metal magazines like Canada's *Metallion* or the UK's *Metal Forces*, and they would trade demo tapes of new and upcoming bands. Langevin explains: "Yeah, we were able to send cassettes of our demo — we recorded a live tape at the jam space and it was called *To the Death 84*. It was re-released last year by Alternative Tentacles, actually, and we sent it to fanzines, to labels, and we had a friend that had a lot of pen pals in the trading tape mailings of the early eighties who sent it everywhere as well, and at first we got an offer to be part of a compilation on Metal Blade called *Metal Massacre.* The Metal Massacre compilations were the start for many of our peers like Slayer, Celtic Frost, Possessed, so we were really happy to have a deal for one song on a compilation, and the reaction was really good. The same year we got an offer for a full album. What happened was we borrowed $2,000 from Snake's mom, which we gave back years later, so we were able to record our first album in a couple of days."

One of the biggest promotional perks of a record deal in the eighties and early nineties involved a budget to produce a music video. For bands that had pounded the Trans-Canada in an effort to bring their music and image to the people, a video was a means (albeit a potentially expensive one) to spread their hard rock gospel to hundreds of thousands, if not millions of teens hungry for music videos. As I mentioned before, MuchMusic's *Power Hour* was *the* go-to source for all things hard and heavy, and I was curious to get the perspective of someone who was involved with delivering the metal goods to the masses.

Craig Halket began his career at MuchMusic during a work placement in 1985, hanging out with the first cast of VJs who would infiltrate the basements of countless suburban Canadian homes, personalities like J.D. Roberts, Laurie Brown, Michael Williams, Christopher Ward, and Erica Ehm. He went on to start at MuchMusic full-time in 1986 as a production assistant, then as a floor manager and producer. He started programming in the eighties and then became a VJ. Craig ultimately became the head of music programming in 2000.

"I think [heavy metal videos] were a huge priority," says Halket. "*Power Hour* was one of our flagship shows, certainly when I started there, and continued to be right through to the mid-nineties. It was a number one priority. We basically interviewed every sort of metal band that came through — Judas Priest, Iron Maiden, and newer bands as well that were sort of breaking out when you had the explosion of Mötley Crüe and Poison [in the mid- to late-eighties]."

And what were the Canadian hard rock or heavy metal bands that stood out in Craig's mind?

"To me, there were a few. I mean, certainly Helix was a band that to me kind of just stood out because the videos were consistent and also back in those days when they had a record release party, there was a lot of fanfare. There was a lot leading up to it, so I think that band certainly stood out in a big way. They kind of dominated in terms of a really hard rock band. I mean, you had your Honeymoon Suites and bands like that, but I think that Helix was pure unadulterated hard rock/heavy metal and they were a dominant force on the *Power Hour*. And then as you got through the late eighties and early nineties, you had [Hamilton, Ontario's] Varga, Slik Toxik, and Sven Gali, which were also sort of key components of the *Power Hour*."

Did Craig notice certain trends in the stylization of Canadian hard rock and heavy metal videos, as opposed to their American counterparts?

"I think maybe they were a little cleaner. I mean, certainly I think there were a lot of similarities, there's no question that was something that comes with just, you know, us being a country that is so close geographically. I think artistically there was a lot of that and I think certainly for Canadian metal bands, I mean they would have great careers here, but the breakthrough to be able to play in the States and go to L.A. and sort of be discovered there, was a big deal."

So would Craig say there was an aspiration towards American-style production values?

"Absolutely. I think that there was a big deal about following the sound trends. I think that certain bands had a distinct sound but ultimately they were always going to be compared to American artists, so I think that there were a lot of similarities."

As a fan, I always wondered if the hosts of the *Power Hour* and later the *Power 30* were fans of the heavy metal genre, or were they just fulfilling one of the job requirements of being a VJ? I mean, both J.D. Roberts and Laurie Brown went on to high-profile, serious newscasting jobs and Michael Williams also hosted MuchMusic's *Soul in the City* show ... were they committed to throwing the horns?

"To me, I think that everyone, whether or not they were huge fans coming in, came out as huge fans. J.D. Roberts certainly was a genuine fan of the music, as was Dan Gallagher — Laurie Brown embraced it. I mean, she was just a fan of all music and a lot of VJs that were at

MuchMusic were into a broad spectrum of music at the time. Teresa Roncon also was definitely into the music. I think that everything in the heavy metal scene, that hard rock scene, was attractive and it was fun, and I think it had the energy. It's an energy that has gone away from music in a lot of ways after the mid-nineties, but I think that everyone was into it. Nobody was just walking through it and just playing a role."

For so many artists who had hauled massive SVT bass rigs and Marshall 4X12 cabinets up flights of icy stairs in the dead of winter, a record deal likely seemed like the endgame, the golden ticket ... a chance to leave the bars and clubs for the luxury of that elusive "big time." In reality, though, a record deal was just the next step up a *very* high ladder, one with many more rungs to climb. It's a big world out there, and while a deal could certainly function as a pipeline to get one's music to the masses, the work really only begins when a contract is signed. In the eighties there was a focus on the part of record label marketing teams to make the acts seem larger than life, that the artists' success was already at hand, and the young audience they targeted were merely invited along to share in the band's excess and glory. In fact, this was the hook that the labels needed to get those allowance dollars, which in turn fuelled the machine, which then generated profit for the label, which would then lay out more dollars that were to be recouped out of the artists' share of the record sales ... tough to buy a mansion and a sports car when you are part of this cycle!

But success can be defined in many ways other than financial, and one wonders if the rewards wrapped up as artistic endeavour or acclaim and notoriety were enough to offset the personal financial realities of the artists.

I think this brings us back to that initial motivation: when music hits you as hard as it hit these artists, you need to be a part of it. It is a desire that is far stronger than the one that pushes you to make "safe" decisions. The very thought of having your emotions and songs committed to wax, to having your face and band logo emblazoned on a record jacket, to having someone actually help you to take the celebration of your lifestyle to other like-minded souls and perform for them in the arenas where *your* heroes had performed can easily be perceived as "making it." And sure, we all know that whatever comes up must come down ... but before we worry about gravity, let's take a look at the achievement of escape velocity, when the artists were able to break the Earth's gravitational pull and touch some of those stars that had previously existed only in their eyes.

the BoRdeR: CANADIANS takiNg HeAVy Metal to the WoRld

"Born and bred in the Great White North, we metalheads bene-fitted from a vast array of bands and styles that helped shape the scene throughout the world."
— Metal Tim Henderson, *Brave Words and Bloody Knuckles*

Sometimes I wish that I hadn't spent so much time in class daydream-ing about being a rock star and hanging out with my heavy metal heroes. As I sit here trying to describe the artistic desire to take one's music to the world, I struggle to think of some parallel between a great explorer, a tale of Magellan or Columbus or some other soul who set out into the great unknown in the name of adventure, profit, and conquest. But screw me if I can, because I spent most of my time in history class doodling intricate diagrams of arena lighting trusses, working on band logos on my weathered binder, or perfecting my Mötley Crüe-inspired pentagrams on a pencil case. Suffice it to say that a life devoted to the pursuit of heavy metal in all its permutations can leave one with serious gaps in conventional knowledge.

As a boy spending summers up at my cottage north of Témiscaming, Quebec, I was fascinated with my cousin's CB radio kit. Because we were deep in the woods, we were able to pick up radio stations from all across North America due to the lack of airwave interference you'd experience in a big city. By the same token, we were also able to use that CB kit to communicate with a variety of truckers as they thundered along Highway 101, delivering wood chips from Tembec, the huge international pulp-and-paper mill that was the foundation of the town of Témiscaming proper. To me, it was amazing that I could have the power to communicate my thoughts and ideas across these invisible airwaves, crackling with life (c'mon, I'm not gonna reference Rush in a Canadian music book?). In the same way that reading the DC and Marvel comics that I collected in my youth made me long to visit the massive skyscrapers and bustling streets of the ink-coloured version of America that was painted in my head, I also longed to have my voice reach people all around the world. In retrospect, I believe that the act of reaching out to people and engaging them in the name of community was equally as important to me as any message I wanted to convey. Who cares what we're saying, as long as we're saying it together! How Marshall McLuhan of me!

So, reaching out beyond the limitations of my environs in the hopes of connecting with other like-minded souls in exotic locales was definitely a goal of mine as a musician. In the pre-Internet, Cold War-obsessed eighties, my image of people other than North Americans, Europeans on the "right" side of the Iron Curtain, and the purportedly West-obsessed Japanese, was coloured by what American TV was feeding me. But in my heart I always believed that there were Commie kids who wanted to rock just as hard as I did, and I dreamed of one day bringing the massive stages I was designing on those scraps of paper to the U.S.S.R. or Communist China to liberate the youthful masses with high-voltage hair metal. Maybe I also figured that since these people were denied their basic right to rock, my own meagre attempts at songwriting might seem like strokes of genius to a metal-starved market! I also became obsessed with becoming "Big in Japan," a dream largely inspired by my obsession with Cheap Trick's *Live at Budokan* album. Hey, anything looks cool when it has Japanese writing on it, right? I always felt there was a good shot that my fortunes lay outside of the borders of my country.

Of course, as time went on, I realized that music fans around the world share a common characteristic. They by and large want great music, and if your music isn't knocking them dead in Ottawa, it probably won't be knocking them dead in Tokyo. As the quality of my own writing and performance improved, doors opened both at home and in the U.S., Europe, and Japan. With my band Crash Kelly, I was afforded the opportunity to tour the UK with The Quireboys and the U.S. with Alice Cooper, performing in front of large crowds with varying degrees of success. I have also seen my albums released throughout North America, Europe, and Japan. Fortunately, we were never booed off a stage, but I have most definitely endured my share of middle finger salutes, downturned thumbs, and shrugged shoulders from restless concertgoers anxious to see the main attraction. Such is the lot of the support act.

However, one thing that I felt kept Crash Kelly afloat, and in many cases even won us some supporters, was that we felt genuinely privileged to be bringing our Canadian (albeit heavily influenced by English glam rock and American hair metal) rock 'n roll to foreign audiences. In these moments, I always felt like I was living out the role of the lucky fan who got to live his dreams more so than a "rock star." I also felt extremely honoured to be representing my country on the world stage. The thrill of playing legendary venues such as Rock City in Nottingham, England, King Tut's Wah Wah Hut in Glasgow, Scotland, the Ryman Auditorium in Nashville, Tennessee, or the Sturgis Bike Rally in North Dakota were never lost on me or the band. It is also hard to explain the thrill of walking into an HMV in London, England, or the famed Tower Records (RIP) on L.A.'s Sunset Strip and finding your albums racked alongside those of your heroes.

I often heard from promoters, local crews, and the headline acts we supported that there was a certain something, a humility and a graciousness about Canadian bands, that made them fun to work with, and this was something that stuck with me. I felt it a badge of honour that I had to defend. While I would certainly never generalize and say that all Canadian bands were like this, I decided, rightly or wrongly, that the public face of Crash Kelly would exude the polite, meek, humble nature that is so often associated with Canadians. Undoubtedly, this got us pushed around at times ... not a very rock 'n roll thing to admit. But ultimately, our humility won us the respect of many of the bands we worked with. We saved our rock star behaviour for the stage (or backstage, behind closed doors!) and flew the flag high for Canadian manners. We practised the attitude of gratitude.

But of course, that was us. Canada has many more attributes besides our perceived good manners. And I have always wondered what the Canadian rockers who inspired me thought of their own Canadian identities as they pertained to their musical identities outside of Canada.

When I asked Lips about touring abroad, he felt strongly that where he and Anvil were from influenced how others perceived his band.

"Oh yeah, that was definitely part of the equation, a very important part in a certain sense because what separates you [from other bands] is where you're from. Metal is metal, but it does matter where you are from. That's sort of what got us labelled as 'The band Anvil from Canada' rather than just Anvil. The second part of your label is where you're from."

Was being Canadian just a form of classification, or did it have deeper ramifications? Do metal musicians bring something unique to their music that actually informs the music itself?

"What your country is and your background seems to somehow permeate the music. I really can't explain why or how, but it just does. Certainly the bands from England had a different kind of way of expressing themselves as far as their lyrics were concerned. The lyrics seemed to have ... maybe the rhymes were better? There was just something about it that you could tell they were English. Maybe it's better diction, I guess. But there were other things, certain musical modes that a lot of the bands play in. I think it's cultural in a certain sense with British bands. A lot of the modes were in minor keys and stuff like that, odd and even dissonant modes like Black Sabbath. These were unusual things for American-sounding bands. A lot of American bands, everything was very square or round in the sense that they didn't use dissonant notes and most of songs were not written in minor keys. They were more blues- oriented chord changes. Europeans seemed to use a lot of classical changes in their music, whereas North Americans didn't. Classical music coming from Europe ... it was kind of the same thing as their metal, you know?"

Brighton Rock toured all throughout the U.S. and Europe, support-
ing the likes of Joan Jett, Eddie Money, and Eric Martin (who would
later go on to front virtuosic hitmakers Mr. Big), and in his travels Gerry
McGhee was well aware of the perception of his band as "Canadian" in
the eyes of foreign markets.

"Yeah, yeah, there definitely was that perception, and I think that's
what appealed more to the European market, the same way that a lot of
European bands broke here in Canada before they ever broke America,
you know? Supertramp, Genesis, Pink Floyd, those guys were all selling a
million records in Canada before they'd even sold anything in the States.
Canada's always kind of had that openness to prog rock, and openness
to bands like Whitesnake and Thin Lizzy. All those kind of bands broke
here first. In the UK, they felt that we had a distinctive Canadian sound.
I mean, we [Gerry's company, Isotope Records] still sell Brighton Rock
records over there regularly, we sell Coney Hatch, Max Webster, Rush,
of course. You'd be surprised how much demand there is for Canadian
rock. The Amazons of the world and the Internet have opened things up
for these people to buy the stuff, and it still sells."

There are two schools of thought regarding the stereotype of the
well-mannered and polite Canadian abroad as pertains to heavy metal
and hard rock musicians. Some musicians feel and embrace that perception, while others don't think it makes one iota of difference.

Perhaps it was a touch of Canadian charm that helped White Wolf
vocalist Don Wolf and band turn a potentially rough situation into a
positive one on an early U.S. promo trip.

"Any time a band is on the road, situations can arise," says Wolf. "You
have to understand that in the eighties things were still somewhat unde-
veloped as far as tolerance for long-haired guys down in the southern
part of the U.S., and we had many looks and comments from people at
the truck stops along the way on our U.S. tour in 1985. One thing that
came to mind that started off a little scary but ended up well was when
we first went to New York for three days of interviews for both magazines and TV. We were taken out for dinner by one of our record people

at RCA and they drove us to a restaurant in Little Italy, and this place looked like it was right out of one of the movies of the time.

"It was this small, not modern room with almost no one there. I think the name of the restaurant was Rugero's ... well, as we walked in there were these two huge, and I mean huge guys standing at the door, and the last thing we heard as we were led in to the back of this place was 'Make sure that these guys pay.' Huge swallow.

"Well, we went in, got seated and started to order ... they had a guy that wandered throughout the restaurant, playing a guitar and singing ... well, as he got to our table, he asked who we were. We explained, and he was overjoyed that we were from Canada and proceeded to sing to us. Well, I happened to know a bit of the song and started to sing with him and pretty soon a bunch of us joined in. On hearing this, the actual owner came out wondering what the noise was about, ended up sitting down with us, spending part of the evening with us, and we ended up signing a bunch of pics and records for him and his kids, and even had the big burly guys hanging out with us and having a blast that night. We had a great dinner, and we remained friends with the owner and contacted him next time we were back in New York. It all ended very well!"

Killer Dwarfs did a substantial amount of touring abroad with acts like Accept, Krokus, and the Michael Schenker Group, but most memorable among those experiences was being the support slot on a few legs of Iron Maiden's tour in support of their prog-metal opus *Seventh Son of a Seventh Son*. Not only did the Dwarfs get to support the band in the U.S., they were also invited to perform in Maiden's backyard in the UK, which included appearances at the famed Wembley Arena and the Hammersmith Apollo. Not only did their personification of the stereotype of Canadians as easygoing, nice guys help them earn fans, it also helped them develop friendships with some legendary heavy metallers.

"I think it's the classic story with everybody that loves Canadians [abroad]," says Russ Dwarf. "I think that initially people thought we were American and then all of a sudden they discovered, oh, they're Canadian guys. We always got along with everybody. And honestly, it's not like you have the cure for cancer or something. You're in show business, you're entertaining people, and the great thing is you can touch people. I always call it plucking the heartstrings of humans — you can touch them and do a show and people come up to you and say 'Oh man, that song changed my life.' That's a great thing, man. It's kind of like a little cure for depression or something. Everybody was pretty outgoing [in the band] and we never had a problem with people. Iron Maiden ended up being lifelong friends, and [the Seventh Son tour] was one of the greatest experiences for us, for sure. They're just great guys, down-to-earth people."

Iron Maiden founder and generally acknowledged leader Steve Harris has a much-documented love of Canadian hard rock and has often tipped his cap to acts like Coney Hatch (who supported Maiden in North America on the Piece of Mind tour) and Kim Mitchell. As Carl Dixon suggests, a combination of being great guys as well as great musicians can open a lot of doors.

"Yeah, if there's a leader of that band [Iron Maiden] of course it's him. And he decided that he liked us and was quite involved in getting us on their tour, I think. He's stayed friends with Andy Curran over the years since then. Whenever I have come across Steve in the years since he has been very friendly and welcoming, and that certainly is another example of what they always say in this business, it's about who you know or it's about your connections. A connected guy like Steve Harris decided that he liked us. Therefore when Coney Hatch was put before him, he opened the door to let us be part of his world."

In the case of Helix, the additional muscle of having major record company support helped the band pay the hefty fee required to "buy on" to the European leg of KISS's Lick It Up tour of 1983. This tour was historically significant for metal fans (or KISS fans anyway!) because it marked the first time that the band had appeared live without their trademark makeup.

"I think Capitol paid something like $30,000 dollars to get us on that tour. One of the funniest stories from that tour involved Mark Rector, who was playing bass. We had brought him in last-minute because Mike Uzelac had quit, and, as I say in my book, Mark wasn't the sharpest knife in the drawer. We were landing for the first date in Lisbon, Portugal, and Mark's looking out the window and I remember him saying, 'This doesn't look like England.' England? We're in fucking Portugal, man! Why would you think we're in England?

"Our next date after that was in Spain and the band all went ahead — they drove, but I had to take a train because I was doing promo. It was called the Lusitania Express. As you drove through the countryside you could see where during the Spanish Civil War they strafed the walls with machine guns and some frigging guy with a machine gun, an army guy, would come wake us up every half-hour … talk about a nerve-wracking ride! They were waking you up to check your passport and shit. Then I got to Madrid and I just figured somebody would know English, but nobody did and there were gypsies yanking on me. I got in a cab and, unbeknownst to me, KISS had changed the hotel. So the name of the hotel I had was wrong. The taxi driver knew where KISS was staying so he took me to the right hotel and out back there was this huge pit, like a garbage pit behind the hotel, and there would be dump trucks constantly pulling up and dumping garbage. And then you'd see about thirty little gypsy kids flock into the garbage and pick through it."

Culture shock aside, I had to wonder how the mammoth rock machine that was KISS treated the support act.

"Well, I get along with the guys in the band, don't get me wrong. But we never got a sound check on that whole tour. And as I said, I think Capitol paid like $30,000 U.S. to get us on that tour."

Turns out a hefty fee for the support slot wasn't the only promotional challenge faced by Helix on this, their first European jaunt.

"We put posters up [in the arena] that the record company had brought out and Gene Simmons made us take them all down. Gene had a little meeting with us too at the first gig. He sat us all down and said, 'You know, no one wants another KISS. Quit using our moves and stuff … or else.' I can't even remember now, maybe we *were* [stealing stage moves] [laughs]. Well, because we used to sit there and watch the headliners and study them, and we would make notes and we discussed them as a band, just how they talked to the audience slower, articulated more, so in that regard … but it wasn't like we were stealing a direct frigging thing off them. We were taking what they were doing and kind of using it to improve our show. I can't remember what he was specifically referring to, but I remember him lecturing us like we were in grade one and he was the head school-teacher. I remember one day Gene did the devil horn hand gesture thing, and he's pointing to himself, and I go, 'I don't get it, what are you telling me?' [laughs] He says, 'Me. I invented that.' I go, 'Oh yeah.' And then I think that's why Ronnie James Dio says, 'Fuck him, he did not!' [laughs]"

Vollmer's encounters with Simmons were not the only ones that remain vivid in his mind ... two legendary characters from the UK band Motörhead, Lemmy Kilmister and Brian "Robbo" Robertson (perhaps more famously known as one half of the classic guitar duo in Thin Lizzy) both remain indelibly inked on Brian's brain, albeit for different reasons.

"Well, there's lots of stories with Lemmy. I remember one night we all watched him get a blow job on the roof of the Penny Arcade [a club in Rochester, NY]. The first time I ever talked to Lemmy was actually that same day. A lot of things happened that day. First off, Robbo tried to beat me up at the fucking House of Guitars [a musical instrument store in Rochester]. But then later on I was sitting there eating lunch and Lemmy was sitting there eating beside me and I had never talked to him before ever, and he turned to me and goes, 'Do you believe in God?' And I go, 'Yeah.' [growling] 'I don't believe in God. My father is a preacher....' And then he started talking about being a roadie for Jimi Hendrix and how they both did acid and were stoned for like two or three days!

"So anyway, we were at the House of Guitars to thank them for selling our first two independent albums. When we were with Motörhead's *Another Perfect Day Tour*, it was in support of *No Rest for the Wicked*. So we were down there and they showed up two hours late for their in-store appearance, and Robbo was pissed. In fact, he had a 40-ouncer of vodka with him, right, and all these kids are standing around. There were like 200 kids. And he was fucked. Anyway, he was obviously pissed and everybody there was kind of laughing because he was so drunk that he was staggering. And I made the mistake of saying, 'Hey, Robbo, having a bad day?' Suddenly with lightning speed he just grabbed me by the throat. I didn't know what to do. Everybody went quiet. It was one of those 'you could hear a pin drop' moments. Everybody was standing around and he said, 'You'd be fucking drunk too if you found somebody fucking your old lady.' And then he kind of looked around and realized everybody was looking at us so he let me go. It was wild."

Helix would make a big mark in the U.S. with the heavy rotation airplay of their "Heavy Metal Love" video on MTV and the radio success of subsequent hits like "Rock You" and "Deep Cuts the Knife." The band also proved itself an arena-worthy support act, winning over American stadium audiences by warming up the crowd for acts like Whitesnake, Quiet

Riot, Black Sabbath, Dio, Mötley Crüe, and Heart. The tour with Heart, in support of the *No Rest for the Wicked* album, was bassist Daryl Gray's inauguration into the band. It was also his initiation into the types of troubles that can await a musician as he crosses the border with a rock band.

"Monday night we go catch the tour bus in Kitchener to head down to Garry, Indiana, to play with Heart. And of course the bus breaks down before it even gets out of Kitchener — the story of Helix's life. We end up having to fly, so we get to Toronto and of course U.S. immigration has a desk in Toronto and I get called up. 'Daryl Gray?' 'Yes.' 'Have you ever been arrested?' 'No.' 'Are you sure?' 'Yeah, I'm pretty sure of that.' [laughs] 'You've never been arrested for sex crimes.' 'No.' 'Go take a seat over there.' So I go sit down. In the meantime, the band is on the plane and Kenny the tour manager is going, 'What the hell is going on here?' The guy they had auditioned a couple before me had been turned away at the border because he had a record.

"So they call me up again and they're looking at my passport and going, 'So you were born in Ireland?' I give them all the information and they tell me to go sit down again. So I go sit down again. And then about two minutes before they're going to lock the door to the plane they call me back up and say, 'Okay, you're okay to go.' Later my mum found an article in the Toronto paper saying a guy called Daryl Gray had escaped from a Michigan prison and they found him and his buddy about three days later. They followed him to a cesspool where he couldn't get out. The buddy had died but this guy Daryl Gray had clung onto the side of the cesspool in the prison break and they were just checking to make sure it wasn't the same Daryl Gray.

"We get to Gary, Indiana, at five o'clock, and of course we've got one instrument each because we're only allowed to bring one. We're on at 7:30. The Heart guys take us aside and say, 'Listen, we heard that you had some problems and you might need some spares…. These ones are our spare-spares, and if you'd like to borrow one of them for the show till your gear gets here tomorrow, feel free.' An excellent band to tour with. The crew was always miserable, as every crew is, but miserable in a fun kind of way [laughs]."

The next night of the Heart tour in Louisville, Kentucky, would see a famous pair of Dutch brothers bringing some levity and a few words of wisdom.

"So we get through the first half of the set, we come to Brent's guitar solo, and Paul and me are off the side of the stage and we hear the audience start to go absolutely nuts, they're going bananas, and we're going, 'Brent's having a good solo tonight. Behind Brent where he can't see is Eddie Van Halen with one of Nancy Wilson's acoustic guitars. As Brent is doing the hammer-ons in his guitar solo [a technique made famous by Eddie], Eddie is doing the same thing behind him. The audience is going nuts and Brent is going 'Aw yeah, this is it!' [laughs] Then Eddie runs off and Brent doesn't find out till later what was going on! Van Halen was in town the next night at whatever the big football stadium is in Louisville. Eddie and Alex came out to see Heart but they spent the whole set in our dressing room just talking with us. One of the best quotes that I can remember is Alex telling me, 'Listen, you can't go chasing the pot of gold, you've just gotta ride the rainbow.'"

To compound the stress of this near-miss of the first date of the Heart tour, this was also to be Daryl's first major venue performance! I can tell you from personal experience, like so many things in life, there is nothing like that first time ... the adrenaline rush is something that musicians chase their entire career, but it is hard to capture or put into words the first time the lights go down in the house and you hear your band's name being introduced to thousands of pumped-up rock fans.

So here you are, you find you've gone from playing in clubs to your first big show, the huge audience is screaming for your every lick and well-choreographed stage move. And now you are going to do it night after night in arenas and theatres across that land of milk and honey which is the US of A! Surely you are travelling in style and living the high life, right?

"Far from it! First of all we did a bunch of little mini-tours before *Razor's Edge* came out." says Daryl Gray. "We'd go out for six or seven shows with Heart or doing our own bar dates, then come back. At that point Helix wasn't playing bars in Canada any more. But we were doing some dates basically to keep the band hot and to crowd-test new material. So when *Razor's Edge* came out in May of '84, we were gearing up to go on the road full-time. By this time the band had its own bus, which was a converted Bluebird Diesel called The Dirty Dog because it looked kind of nice on the outside but it was a hound. It had a little piece at the back that our stage gear could fit in, and it didn't have a nice washroom like the rest of the tour buses had.... Our first string of dates was forty-seven shows in forty-seven days, and we didn't take accommodations; there were no rooms because we were driving overnight. I remember playing, I think it was the Boat House in Norfolk, Virginia, right behind Norfolk Navy Yard. It was really an old warehouse on the dock that they converted into a rock bar. To shower that day they had a standpipe outside that basically served for hosing down the old dockside, so you cranked the big turn handle on, ice cold water, and that was your shower for the day. And occasionally we would get a shower room, but basically the band had made a conscious decision that we weren't going to take tour support, because we didn't want to owe everything that ever came in to the record company. So we made sure that what money was made from touring supported the touring."

So much for the glamour ... but what the hell, personal comfort is a small price to pay for living one's rock 'n roll fantasies abroad!

In the cases of Voivod and Anvil, touring abroad provided a bedrock that has sustained the careers of both bands for decades. Anvil was aided by Attic Records president Al Mair's solid relationship with Doug Smith, who managed the legendary Motörhead, as well as early eighties metal mainstays Girlschool, and tours with both acts were the result of this friendship. Mair was also instrumental in getting the band a slot on the bill for Japan's massive Super Rock Festival, which saw Anvil standing toe-to-toe with such metal giants as Scorpions, Whitesnake, and the Michael Schenker Group. That festival also featured a little-known New Jersey band in the support slot by the name of Bon Jovi. It was Europe, however, that yielded the greatest return on time invested.

Lips: "Oh yeah, Europe. We made a huge impact in Europe, massive, in fact, to the point where it kept the band a recording band for thirty plus years since."

And was there something distinctly Canadian about Anvil that appeared to European audiences?

"We were unique. In the early eighties, you had to have a sound and a style that was your own. Otherwise you didn't get a record deal. So that is why, as well as being Canadian, we have kept that throne all through the years, to this day. People know that Anvil is a Canadian band, and part of our marketing is that. By the time we did our fifth album, we had a song called 'Blood on the Ice,' not that dissimilar from your book [laughs]. Many years later, probably in '97 or '98, the record company and promotional company decided to make a T-shirt that looked like a hockey jersey and put '98' on the back with Blood on the Ice and the Canadian maple leaf on the front with the Anvil logo over top in white. It looked like a white hockey jersey, and when we played the Wacken Festival in Germany in '98 we probably sold a thousand. And part of it had to do with the Canadian maple leaf. We've got a number of different T-shirt designs that we use to this day that all have the Canadian insignia. I mean, it becomes part of it. I wear something with the Canadian insignia on it onstage every night — whether it's wristbands or a T-shirt, there's always something indicating it's Lips from Anvil from Canada. It's funny, because we have a song on our latest album (*Juggernaut of Justice*) called 'Fuckin' Eh.' And now we've changed the Blood on the Ice shirt to a Fuckin' Eh shirt. It's become part of the show. Steve-O [from MTV's *Jackass*] came up to me at a show in Los Angeles at the House of Blues and said, 'Hey Lips, do you know how to spell Canada?' And I go, 'Huh?' And he goes, 'C -eh-N-eh-D-eh.' [laughs]. And that's become part of the show. I talk about being Canadian. I even talk about being the Stompin' Tom Connors of heavy metal. I play a few bars of a couple of his songs, and it really goes over very, very well worldwide. Our management goes, 'We don't see how these Blood on the Ice shirts or Fuckin' Eh shirts are gonna sell.' Meanwhile, they're selling like hotcakes in Germany."

Voivod's Michel Langevin: "The first U.S. tour with Celtic Frost was quite an experience. We barely knew English and our lyrics were pretty funny on the first couple of albums, but we really learned touring, especially in the U.S. So the first tour in '86 with Celtic Frost was an amazing experience and we learned a lot from it. And then we did this crazy world tour. Actually, the same year we toured Europe with Possessed and it was equally insane because those were the big thrash metal years with huge crowds and huge mosh pits and riots and all that. It was very exciting because all of these bands were touring, like we did a world tour in '87 with Creator, and we were all young kids, you know? And thrash metal was exploding and it was very exciting for everybody. I think that the biggest thrill was 1990 when we toured *Nothingface* — we first went across the U.S. with Faith No More and Soundgarden and shortly after we did a Canadian tour with Rush, which was pretty amazing."

As French-Canadian musicians, did Voivod ever feel that they were perceived differently by their peers both in the rest of Canada and internationally?

"Sort of, in the sense that we were on a parallel path because being here in Quebec and singing in English kept us from being part of the Quebec scene in a way. And the fact that we were French Canadian might have kept us from being part of the Canadian scene, but then again I'm not sure of it, because we did get nominated for both Junos and ADISQ here. So I think we were pretty well respected, but many people, in terms of recognition, many people know the name Voivod but they don't exactly know the music. It's more of a specialized thing to like Voivod. It's still an underground phenomenon in a way."

Playing live was one part of the equation involved in getting one's music heard in lands foreign and afar, but the real shot at musical immortality in other countries lay in the much anticipated and desired Foreign Territory Release, a situation that would hopefully see an artist's recording distributed, marketed, and promoted in specific regions. However, this could be a precarious situation and certainly not as easy as it would seem, even for artists with "worldwide" deals. Harry Hess sheds some light on the fiscal realities of this from his own experience with Harem Scarem.

"On the first record we got Spain and Portugal, I think, outside of Canada. And that was it. So what would happen was we would make the record here domestically and then it was up to the international marketing manager here in Canada to solicit the finished record to the international counterparts. So they would hit up the international marketing managers in Spain and Japan. With a band like us coming out of Canada, and this is what I found later on in life [laughs], is that we were as seriously disadvantaged as any Canadian band signed to a major label in Canada would be moving forward, but you don't know that at the time ... because the international marketing manager, let's say in Spain or the UK, or Japan, would be looking at taking on bands and releasing them in their territories that have done really big numbers. Because as you know it's all about selling records and numbers. How can you do that in Canada, a territory where there are no people, comparing it to the States? So if the marketing manager in Spain was looking at taking on, let's say two or three international projects that they were going to work in their country, it was always going to be the American ones because they were supported by huge numbers. The resources behind the U.S. acts that were signed domestically in America ended up being the Poisons and Ratts ... they all had numbers that totally crushed ours. So if in Canada you even said that you had a gold-certified album [50,000 units], well what is that compared to selling five million records in America? So you were behind the eight-ball with regard to getting any type of look from a lot of international territories other than the one that you were signed in.

"The guarantee [of release] was only for the territory you were physically signed in, which for us was Canada, obviously. So that was the challenge, and nobody really explained that to me when we signed the record deal. No matter who it is, you can really attribute the struggle of any Canadian major label artist to the sheer fact that if you're signed in Canada there is no incentive for the international counterparts to take on your records from a monetary perspective, because they take a discounted rate when they take on another territory's product. That alone is huge incentive for them to just work their own stuff. It's in their [the foreign territory's] best interest to work their own product that they signed and they have an investment in. So it always felt to me like there was an underlying nudge and a wink of, 'Oh yeah, we'll look at it and we'll see what we can do,' but the cycle of recording and releasing meant they wouldn't even hear our record sometimes until six months after it had already been released domestically. So really, the only way that a band could break from one territory to the next at that time was if you were doing huge, huge numbers in your own territory. And again, how can that be impressive if you're from Canada?"

So, with the cards stacked so high against you, what is the point of even trying to reach out to an international audience? It certainly isn't a wise move if you base your decision on numbers alone.

The difference here is the "business" we are dealing with. We are not talking about widgets, we are talking about music, and music brings another dimension into play. The ability to reach out and communicate with a listener in a truly resonant way makes this business a special one, and the music industry is built on the leaps of faith taken by music executives who were touched by the seemingly intangible. It is so easy to forget that when you are studying the numbers. The connective strand of all those power chords, double-bass drum fills, and soaring vocals have moved people to believe that heavy rock music from Canada can succeed in foreign lands. Fortunately for Harem Scarem, someone believed that the music brought forth on their second record, *Mood Swings*, was strong enough to warrant a roll of the dice, and the gamble paid off.

"If you fast forward to our second record, a new guy took on the international marketing manager job at Warner Music Canada, and because it was his new position, he was like, 'Wow, I think I better do something.' So he started sending it out everywhere and trying to get international releases, and by our second record he could say, 'Well we did this in Canada, we had x amount of singles charting, we sold this amount of records, here's the new record. It's a little more heavy, a little more in keeping with what's happening at radio right now.' And Japan took interest in it.

"When Japan decided they liked that record, we were touring in Edmonton at the time and I got a fax from the label saying, 'Hey, got you released in Japan,' and we were like, 'Wow, that's amazing,' because we always looked at bands that were selling records internationally and we thought that was another level. Touring the world, selling records around the world, that's really, really cool ... really nothing had happened at that point, but then then we just started getting all kinds of feedback from Japan and started doing interviews and literally got offered a publishing deal from a Japanese publisher. Things started to happen very, very quickly once Japan came on board because [they] controlled a lot of the stuff that happened in Southeast Asia. So if you got Japan, Thailand, Malaysia, Singapore, all those other territories automatically released your record. So we went from getting three releases, including Canada, on our first record, to I think forty releases for *Mood Swings*, our second. It was pockets of Europe, but it was all Asia.

"On the back of Japan liking it and putting it out, we started selling a lot of records there ... as Canada started to move in another direction musically, once *Nevermind* by Nirvana came out, we were dead in the water here as far as radio went, and even the label's interest in the band. Nobody really paid attention to what we were doing, or cared. We went through a bunch of A&R guys at the time. Fortunately, the guy who really signed us was Dave Tollington, the vice president ... I had a direct rapport with the VP and we kind of just kept moving forward, you know? At the end of it all, we just finished our contract. We had a seven-album deal and we finished it. We sold well over a million records during our time with Warner, probably over half in Japan alone, and it was great. And it all started because that international marketing manager in Canada passed it along to Japan, and Japan happened to think that they could do something with it, and they did. If it weren't for that, we never would have gotten past that second record."

While Slik Toxik didn't duplicate the Canadian gold-certified success of their *Doin' The Nasty* album in the U.S., the band still managed to secure a major release south of the border through Capitol Records, which led to support slots with Faster Pussycat and Yngwie Malmsteen. These opportunities not only won fans for the band, they also gave a young and cocksure Nick Walsh the opportunity to show what he was made of musically with one of the world's greatest electric guitar players.

"It was funny because we were two or three days in and nobody had even gotten the opportunity to speak to Yngwie, because he was like the untouchable 'rising force.' [laughs] So the first day we played in Cincinnati, Ohio, with him and everybody just stayed away from him, but we made sure by the end of the day to find out what his favourite beverage was. Our road manager went out and bought a 40-ouncer of Absolut Lemon Citron just to sort of break the ice, you know? We gave that to him, and we heard he was appreciative, oooh.

"So a couple of days go by and we're in Grand Rapids, Michigan. We're at sound check and we all happen to arrive at the same time. We're in front of the stage while the Yngwie guys are getting ready to sound check. And my band was a bunch of chickens. They were afraid of this guy, everybody was all intimidated. And me, I'm like that little tiny Jack Russell terrier that doesn't care who he's barking at, you know what I mean? [laughs] So I go right up to the stage and I go, 'Yo, Yngwie.' And he goes, 'You talking to me?' And I said, 'Yeah, I'm talking to you, my name's Nick, I'm the singer of Slik Toxik.' And he goes, 'Oh, that Canadian band.' I go, 'Yeah, the Canadian band. Let me get up onstage and sing a song with you.' And he goes, 'You? Want to sing with me?' So I said, 'Sure, man, of course I do.' So he goes, 'Okay.' And everyone was shocked.

"So I get up on the stage and he says, 'You know any of my songs?' So I thought I'd pick a really hard one. I said, 'Does your band know 'You Don't Remember, I'll Never Forget'?" He looks at the drummer, Bo, and tells him to count it in. They're playing and everybody's watching and they're going 'What's gonna happen here?' Well, as soon as I started singing right in Yngwie's face, this big smile came over his face and the next thing you know he's spinning his guitar around his neck, throwing picks out at the band and at the crew, and after that every day it seemed like we were probably one of the few bands ever to get along with Yngwie Malmsteen on tour [laughs]. But that was a pretty crazy tour. That guy is, or was, rather, quite manic, so to speak, with his substance use and just his personality at the time. I don't know what's going on with him these days, but I can say that it was quite a crazy time back in 1992!"

Walsh's recounting of this story has a lot more to do with confidence than cockiness. It is a confidence that is forged in the ability to succeed in a home country that is not the most user-friendly in terms of commercially breaking a young band. The hard work it took for Slik Toxik to succeed in Canada could have left them jaded, but instead it made them grateful for the opportunities to perform with artists they considered to be not only their current peers at the time, but also influences.

"We know that we live in a really big place with hardly anybody in it, and we had to be very good at our craft and what we did, so we weren't really out for competition as opposed to camaraderie when we were out on the road.

"We weren't one of those bands that was like, 'Hey, we're gonna blow away the headliner.' We're fans, man. We were fans of all the bands we ever had the opportunity to play with … I think being Canadian and fans at the same time probably did help, because like I said, we weren't out there to compete and be boisterous and all that stuff. We just knew what we had to do."

There is another component to the story of Canadian hard rock and heavy metal outside of our national border. It is the story of individuals or bands who took their shot at the dream by making a move to the U.S. to cultivate and develop their craft and their music. At the heart of this decision was the concept of perceived opportunity, with America being the neon sign glowing in the distance, the oasis in the desert of the frustration of their hopes and dreams. There was a "scene" happening in the mecca of American entertainment, Hollywood, built on the refinement, co-opting, and general "glamming up" of the hard and heavy music of the early eighties. The warm climate and allure of the Californian lifestyle that was the heart of the Sunset Strip in Hollywood was a magnet for hard rock musicians from all over the U.S. and Canada. New York also had a harder, tougher East Coast version of that scene. Toronto had a similarly inspired movement, an almost perfect blend of L.A.'s pomp and hair metal circumstance and New York's brash leather and FU attitude. These scenes were also mimicked in other major U.S. locales. Even Seattle, the city that would ultimately sound the death knell for the hair metal movement in the early nineties, had its share of flashy metal attitude. Early photos of Alice in Chains and Mother Love Bone (which featured members of Pearl Jam) betray glam metal roots.

Peterborough, Ontario, native Sebastian Bierk, better known to the world as Sebastian Bach, is perhaps the world's most genetically gifted hard rock singer, his golden locks seemingly untouched by time and a voice like manna from rock 'n roll heaven. His move from the Toronto scene to the U.S. to hook up with Detroit rockers Madam X ultimately led to his most famous position as lead vocalist for multimillion-selling rockers Skid Row, a band that topped the U.S. Billboard charts with its sophomore album *Slave to the Grind* and ultimately proved to be the act by which all other acts were measured in the commercial "last kick" of hard rock in the eighties.

I asked my good friend and noted heavy metal journalist Aaron Small to share a brief history of the man he considers to be "Canada's Metal Ambassador."

Although vocalist Sebastian Bach was born in Freeport, Bahamas, he was raised in Peterborough, Ontario, and cut his teeth in Toronto bands Winter Rose and Kid Wikkid. A prominent figure in the local scene, Baz (as he's nicknamed) gained worldwide notoriety when he relocated to New Jersey and joined Skid Row. Their self-titled debut was released in 1989 via Atlantic Records and spawned three hit singles: "Youth Gone Wild," "18 And Life," and "I Remember You." These were songs that fans the world over instantly identified with. The album has since been certified five times platinum in the United States, selling in excess of five million copies. The follow-up, *Slave to the Grind*, was released in 1991 and debuted at #1 on the Billboard charts, spearheaded by much heavier songs including "Monkey Business" and the title track.

Sebastian's success was so great that he appeared on the cover of *Rolling Stone* magazine later that year. As frontman for Skid Row, Bach led his group around the globe, touring with the likes of Bon Jovi, Mötley Crüe, Aerosmith, and Guns N' Roses, in addition to countless headlining gigs of their own. Whether in Los Angeles, London, or Tokyo, Sebastian never forgot his Toronto roots and when the iconic Gasworks on Yonge Street was in danger of being shut down, Baz led a fundraiser to try to save the hallowed institution; sadly, it's no longer around. After one more Skid Row album, 1995's *Subhuman Race*, Sebastian would embark upon a solo career that saw him become a multi-faceted star. That instantly recognizable and absolutely unforgettable voice landed Baz on Broadway, with starring roles in *Jekyll & Hyde* and *The Rocky Horror Picture Show*. The transition to television was seamless with a recurring role on the hit series *Gilmore Girls* as well as numerous appearances on MTV and VH1. A larger-than-life personality with a terrific stage presence, Sebastian Bach may live in the land of the Stars and Stripes, but he carries the Maple Leaf with him wherever he goes.

Add to that list musicians like Dream Theater vocalist James Labrie (a one-time member of Canadian band Winter Rose and for a spell lead vocalist of Coney Hatch), Canadian guitarists Phil X and Jason Hook, who have both made names for themselves in L.A.'s competitive session and live scene (Phil recently replaced a recuperating Richie Sambora for a tour with mega act Bon Jovi, while Hook is currently a member of Five Finger Death Punch, one of the most successful metal acts in recent history), Jason McMaster, Barrie native and lead vocalist with Bonham, Phil Naro of Talas and Peter Criss fame, and a host of others have found success by relocating to the U.S. and hooking up with big-name American bands.

As of this writing, Calgary-born and Toronto-raised guitarist Stacey Blades is the guitarist for multi-platinum U.S. rockers L.A. Guns. This was the band formed by guitarist Tracii Guns, initially the "Guns" in the first incarnation of a little band called Guns N' Roses. The obvious joke about Americans and their love of guns is the elephant in the room here, but in this case I guess we can switch out "Guns" with "Blades," and you can bring a knife to a gunfight! Anyway, prior to his stint with L.A. Guns, Blades' first U.S. musical adventure was with a Virgin Records act called Roxx Gang. So what prompted Blades to head down south in 1992, after a few years cutting his teeth in the Toronto scene of the late eighties/early nineties?

"Well, that year they [Roxx Gang] had an ad in *Metal Edge* magazine. Every month there was a new issue and I would always thumb through it. I was downtown at the time and I popped into a bookstore ... and you know, I was a fan of the band. I had their first album, *Things You've Never Done Before*. They were looking for a guitar player and I'm like, *I've gotta get this gig, this is right up my alley*. At that time things were really dying in Toronto ... I don't know why, but bands like Guns N' Roses or L.A. Guns or Roxx Gang or Faster Pussycat or Junkyard, they would never have gotten signed out of Canada. I don't know why the labels always played it safe and didn't really sign any edgy bands.

"There were so many artists that did have record deals in the late eighties and early nineties, but that didn't really even get pushed in the States, so unfortunately I looked at it as like, if I'm going to have a music career, like a *real* music career, I've got to move to America. And getting the Roxx Gang gig ... I responded to the ad, and I talked to their manager and sent them a whole bio and demo and all that stuff, and they called me like two days later. I flew down and nailed the audition and three weeks after that I was on a plane to Florida. In retrospect I'm glad that I did it because it put me on the map, but it was not a good situation. The first few years with the band were pretty cool and then it just kind of went to shit, and it just turned into kind of a nightmare. And then I moved to L.A. and got L.A. Guns, and that was, like, ten years ago. "

Being immersed in the American music scene, I wondered if Blades saw a difference in quality or a reason beyond the fiscal realities outlined by Harry Hess as to why Canadian hard rock and metal didn't break as big as it should have in the U.S.

"You look at Lee Aaron, for example. I was on YouTube the other day and stumbled on one of her old songs. What a great artist. She was Canada's Lita Ford, so to speak. Why wasn't she pushed in the States? She would have sold lots of records; she was a great artist with great songs. It's unfortunate that there are those types of situations, depending on the record deal you got up there [Canada], that really dictated not just how you were perceived in Canada, but were you even known about in the U.S.?"

The machinations of an artist's record deal could be such that forces within your own company could be at work against you. There might be another act on your label's roster that got the push you needed for a multitude of reasons that had nothing to do with the quality of your work.

"I think the last band from Canada to get signed that had some kind of push behind them [from the late eighties/early nineties] in the States was Brighton Rock. I remember they had a big record deal with WEA and I know they got a little push in the States. How well they did down here, I'm not sure. It was weird because all kinds of seventies and early eighties bands, they always got a push in the States, and then something happened from '87 on, and it was just like, 'You're not gonna get known in the States.' So it was frustrating as an up-and-coming musician to see that kind of a reality, and you either went with it or you didn't. You just sucked it up. For myself, I had grander dreams. I said, 'If I'm gonna have a career, I've gotta get out of Canada,' and that's unfortunate to admit because it is a great country."

It really is a numbers game, and obviously with more people to cater to in the U.S., the chance of finding an audience for your music increases. It is important to realize that talent and quality is not always reflected in the number of albums an act sells.

Blades: "So many great bands have come out of Canada. There's too many to mention and it's too bad that looking back, like I was talking about earlier, if the record industry was different — good is good whether it's pop or rock or heavy metal, you know? Good bands with good songs, good is good. Well, why weren't certain artists getting signed, or if they did get signed, why wasn't there just a massive power machine behind them? I think maybe a lot of people from that scene, eventually by '92 or '93, probably just gave up because it's like, this is just too hard. So whether that's a reflection on musicianship or attitudes, I guess maybe, but the cool thing about growing up in Canada is that there's just so many great bands. And yeah, I was into all the American bands as a kid, but if you grew up in Canada and you didn't like Rush there was something wrong with you [laughs]. It's a different staple, so to speak. Like yeah, you grew up on April Wine and Rush and Triumph as a rocker. Of course I listened to Aerosmith and Ozzy and Van Halen and Nazareth and Cheap Trick and The Cars and all that great stuff, but there's a certain little section reserved for you, a VIP section that you must listen to Max Webster and Rush and April Wine and all of those great bands from the seventies. So there's that little niche. It's like we're our own entity and we're our own society, so to speak, being Canadian."

Canadian guitarist Glen Drover, who has made his mark as a guitarist with Megadeth, King Diamond, and Testament, also took what he developed in Canada through his work with his band Eidolon and used that as his "in" to a wider audience.

"When me and Shawn [Drover, Glen's brother] were doing the Eidolon thing, in the early-early nineties, was when he was saying, 'You know, man, look at this band King Diamond' — we were big fans, you know, and the band had only been around for a few years with a string of great records. They kept on going through guitar players, so he said, 'Man, why don't you send a videotape of yourself? Let's film a video of you playing some songs and send it out.'

"At the time they were all based in Europe. That changed later, but they were all in Sweden or Denmark or whatever. So I got in contact with them and their booking agency and sent a videotape and got in contact with King and we hit it off. He liked my style and we became friends, and then an opening came up. That time when I got in with King Diamond was around the time when Eidolon signed to Metal Blade. So I was doing both at the same time, which was really exciting for me — for all of us, actually. And then once I was recommended for the Megadeth gig, it was people who knew the Eidolon stuff and the King Diamond stuff. When I talked to Dave Mustaine, he knew that I had some road experience; he is a Mercyful Fate fan and it kind of went from there. So it was kind of just meeting the right people — I can't really say networking because I was referred, it kind of came out of the blue … I consider myself lucky that I got it, because there's a lot of great musicians here. It's just like any job, I suppose. You just get hooked up with the right people at the right time."

Having worked with a number of successful international artists, does Glen feel there are discernable differences in attitude, character, and approach between Canadian musicians and their American and European counterparts?

"Nah, I don't think so. Not really the culture thing, not really. I mean, I've worked with people overseas as well as with certain people here in Canada, but more so, as you know, more European- and U.S.-based. People that I've dealt with, just thinking of a couple off the top of my head, there's a lot of similarities. Do you get along with somebody? Can you work and move forward and have that common goal and share a certain vision? The whole thing that makes a band work, you hope that you meet people that you can relate to personally and musically, and I've done that pretty much all over the place, so I don't really notice a huge difference. Or I've been lucky about that [laughs]."

Having been blessed in my own personal experiences working with some of the artists who were an influence on me, I couldn't help but inject my love of the music as a fan into my role as a performer and writer. I wondered if Glen felt the same way about he and his brother Shawn's role in Megadeth. Was the band's leader (and original guitarist for metal legends Metallica) Dave Mustaine at all influenced by Glen and Shawn's passion for Megadeth's music?

"Absolutely, are you kidding? Because it was supposed to only be a farewell tour … and it turned into, 'Nah, I'm not putting the band to bed yet.' And I think also too, we were kicking ass. As a unit we worked really well and the fans and the shows, it was definitely — I mean, every place we played man, it was just a lot of electricity. It was very exciting and we did really well on that first tour and I think it put him into a different mindframe, I think, to move forward and not necessarily let the band go. I think he was wanting to do something under his name, more like a solo thing, but we were really more interested in carrying on if it was Megadeth.

"Really, if you call it Dave Mustaine or Megadeth, it really doesn't make a difference in a way because that's him. He *is* Megadeth, as everybody knows. But being part of bringing the band back from the dead and making it really valid and working really well as a unit was what I'm most proud of. It was all for the right reasons and so we were genuinely excited. 'C'mon man, why don't we try this song from that album, remember that one?' It was just heavy excitement. It doesn't happen to many Canadians. There's not a lot of us who have wound up being in a band of this size and not only having that happen, but your brother's there too, and now half the band is Canadian. It's just not something that usually happens, so I was very proud and very happy I was a part of that."

As a musician and a Canadian, one of my proudest moments was performing with Helix at the 2009 Rocklahoma festival in Tulsa, Oklahoma. All of the bands were staying at the Hard Rock Hotel in Tulsa and every night of the festival would end up congregating in the hotel bar, swapping war stories from the road and their illustrious heavy metal pasts. Watching as members of Quiet Riot, Night Ranger, Ratt, Stryper and other major American bands not only recognized but acknowledged and paid respect to the role that Helix played in the eighties heavy metal saga was truly incredible. The night we performed, the bill was Hericane Alice, Helix, Warrant, Night Ranger, and Ratt. In the middle of the afternoon, in blistering 109-degree Fahrenheit temperatures, I'm proud to say we tore the stage apart (even if the heat almost killed lead vocalist Brian Vollmer!). One of my fondest memories is sitting in the crowd enjoying a beer with the Helix drummer at the time, Rob MacEachern, during Night Ranger's set and getting a shout-out from the stage for our performance, and remembering the faces in the crowd singing along during our performances to songs like "Rock You," the song that really kick-started my heavy metal journey. It was amazing to be amongst Canadians making a mark in the U.S., even if it was only for a few hours in the sweltering Tulsa heat.

Steve Shelski, Dave "Thumper" Ketchum, Andy Curran, and Carl Dixon in 1982.

Photo by Patrick Harbron

CONEY HATCH

Carl Dixon of Coney Hatch in full rock-god mode, 1982.

Photo by Jim Prue

Kick Axe in an early live shot with original vocalist Gary Langen.

Kick Axe in full heavy metal regalia. Clockwise from left: Larry Gillstrom, Brian Gillstrom, George Criston, Victor Langen, Raymond Harvey.

Doug Weir and his band Syre, one of Canada's hardest-working road bands.

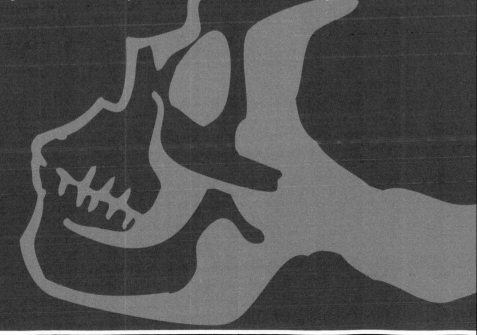

KiLLeR DWaRfS

Clockwise from left: Darrell Millar, Mike Hall, Ronald Mayer, and Russ Graham: The Killer Dwarfs.

DiRTY weAPONS

Tapping into the U.S. market via MTV.

KiLLeR DWaRfS
THE NEW ALBUM
call 1-800-DIAL-MTV to request
DiRTY weAPONS— THE VIDEO
SEE THEM ON TOUR!

CAM MACLEOD   LES SCHWARTZ   DON WILK   LORIS BOLZON   RICK NELSON

A White Wolf promo shot.

WHITE WOLF

STANDING ALONE

HEAVY METAL comes to TOP OF THE ROCK
WEDNESDAY, APRIL 3, 1985
as WHITE WOLF

(AS SEEN ON M-TV) WITH SPECIAL GUEST **EXCALIBUR**

Performing live in concert — Doors open at 7 pm
TICKETS ARE $4.97 IN ADVANCE OR $5.97 NITE OF SHOW

AVAILABLE AT: TICKETMASTER 456-3333
ALL BELIEVE IN MUSICS
TOP OF THE ROCK

K² Concerts

Glenn "Archie" Gamble and the band Vandyl worked the late-eighties Trans-Canada Highway cover band circuit. Gamble later joined Helix.

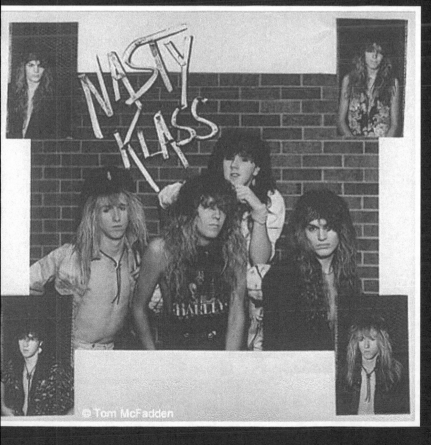

Nasty Klass was one of many Canadian bands that tried to break through by mixing originals and cover songs in Canada's numerous rock bars.

© Tom McFadden

Members of Sword with legendary thrasher James Hetfield.

The late Paul Hackman, Daryl Gray, Brian Vollmer, Brent Doerner, and "Fritz" Hinz: Helix.

"Fritz" Hinz and Brent Doerner of Helix on tour with Tony Iommi and Black Sabbath.

Brian Vollmer sporting the leather look.

A high-flying eighties performance from Helix at the legendary El Mocambo club in Toronto.

Helix's masterful guitar duo tearing it up on the big stage: Brent Doerner and Paul Hackman.

Helix's main writing team of Brian Vollmer and Paul Hackman harmonize onstage.

Brent Doerner of Helix backstage in Kentucky with the eighties' most influential guitarist, Eddie Van Halen.

Who wouldn't want some White Wolf for Christmas?

M.E.A.T

COLLECTORS EDITION * ISSUE#10 * MARCH 1990

CANADA GETS METALLIZED!

FREE FREE

KILLER DWARFS....GET DIRTY

RAZOR....SEEKING OUT JUSTICE

TESTHMENT....RAGE ON TOUR

LEE AARON....SEES PLATINUM

Also In This Issue.....
HARD 'N' HEAVY
JOE SATRIANI
PHIL LEWIS of L.A. GUNS
ATTITUDE / ZERO OPTION

Drew Masters' *M.E.A.T* magazine helped popularize Canadian metal nationally and internationally.

M.E.A.T

FREE!
Issue 31

Canada's #1 Metal Mag!

FREE!
April '92

Nick Walsh of....

Poundin' out a "Nasty" debut!

Inside...A Special
Interview with...
SPINAL TAP
plus....
MR. BIG
MID-EVIL
INFEXIOUS
ENTOMBED
KINGSBANE
GRUNTRUCK
McQUEEN STREET
WAYNE'S WORLD *Giveaway!*

Printed in Canada
pic: Ron Boudreau

Nick Walsh hitting the notes in support of the *Doin' the Nasty* album.

M.E.A.T

FREE!
Issue 33B

FREE!
June '92

Canada's #1 Metal Mag!

Sebastian Bach of...

SKID ROW

"Grind"-ing Through Canada!

Also
In This
Smokin'
Issue!...

IRON MAIDEN

W.A.S.P.
TESTAMENT
SLAUGHTER
JACK DAMAGE

HARDLINE
DEFIANCE
TORA-TORA
MAX SINAGAIN
LOVE JUNCTION
PSYCHOSOMATIC
DEMOLITION HAMMER
MONSTER VOODOO MACHINE

WIN! Prizes for IRON MAIDEN, SKID ROW, SLAUGHTER, TESTAMENT!

Sebastian Bach waved the flag for Canadian metal abroad through his success with chart-topping band Skid Row.

SCOTT WATTS   GUS PYNN   JOE RICO   ROB URBINATI

Sacrifice

SACRIFICE INFORMATION SERVICE (416) 754-4334
c/o B.M. Management
40 Metropolitan Road, Suite 24
Scarborough, Ontario, Canada M1R 2T6

FRINGE
PRODUCT

Sacrifice in an
early promotional
shot for indie
label Fringe.

Denis "Piggy"
D'Amour,
Jean-Yves
"Blacky"
Thériault,
Michel "Away"
Langevin, and
Denis "Snake"
Bélanger of
Voivod.

Lee Aaron delivering one of her patented high-energy shows.

Headpins' Darby Mills shakin' it up.

Darby Mills striking a serious rock pose with the late Brian "Too Loud" McLeod.

Photo by Dee Lippingwell

Holly Woods from the band Toronto in a soulful performance.

Photo by Dee Lippingwell

Holly Woods under the stage lights.

Courtesy of Robert Bursey

Andy Frank in Sven Gali's pre-major label glam rock phase.

Clockwise from left: Kevin Gale, Neal Busby, Pat Howarth, Rob Bruce, and Nick Walsh: Slik Toxik.

Photo by Denise Grant

October 1988

John Rogers   Greg Fraser   Gerald McGhee   Stevie Skreebs   Mark Cavarzan

B R I G H T O N   R O C K

HEAD OFFICE *management*
(416)979-8455

wea Music of Canada, Ltd.

Brighton Rock in 1988.

Gerry McGhee takin' the rock to the Rock in Grand Falls, Newfoundland, 1987.

Ray Coburn, Dave Betts, Johnnie Dee, Derry Grehan, and Garry Lalonde of Honeymoon Suite bringing Canadian rock to *American Bandstand*.

PEPSI

presents

Haywire
Special Guests
Brighton Rock

Wednesday **August 19 1987**	**Grand Falls Stadium**
	$13.00 advance $14.00 day of the show tax included (no refunds) N⁰ 1 0 4 9

A killer double bill in Newfoundland.

Lips of Anvil wowing the new generation of headbangers.

A recent promo shot of Canadian metal ex-pat Stacey Blades.

The versatile Lee Aaron is still a vibrant stage presence.

Voivod's Denis Belanger, still one of metal's most popular festival draws.

Photo by Kevin Lamb

The late, great Dee Cernile, Dave Wanless, and Andy Frank at a Sven Gali reunion show.

Honeymoon Suite's Johnnie Dee.

Photo by Mitch Lafon

Honeymoon Suite's Derry Grehan and Johnnie Dee in full flight.

Sean Kelly commanding the stage with his band Crash Kelly.

Making the Scene

I moved to Toronto in 1991 to attend the Faculty of Music at the University of Toronto, but I have to admit, I had ulterior motives when making that scholastic choice. By the time I was fifteen, I had made a firm decision that a pursuit of the rock 'n roll dream was inevitable, and in fact, it was my destiny. Once that decision was made, I began plotting the ways in which I could make this dream a plausible reality ... or, in other words, I tried to figure out a way to get the hell out of my hometown.

As an avid collector and reader of *Guitar World* magazine, my eyes were constantly drawn to the flashy ads and countless articles touting the glory and glamour of Hollywood, and in particular the Sunset Strip scene. Having heard and romanticized the success stories of bands like Van Halen, Quiet Riot, Mötley Crüe, W.A.S.P., and Ratt in the first half of the eighties, and bands like Poison, Warrant, Bullet Boys, and Bang Tango in the latter half, I obviously looked at Hollywood as my musical mecca (an ideal shared by countless other young musicians, many of whom would go on to prolific careers in the California service industry before succumbing to poverty, homesickness, drug addiction, or some combination thereof).

However, being a cautious young man instilled with a healthy fear of the aforementioned poverty and of bursting the dreams of my parents (I know, not very rock 'n roll), I wanted to find an educational facility that would help me to develop as a musician as well as make the much-needed contacts that would bring me closer to realizing my dream. For this to happen, I needed a big city with a music school and a music scene, and Los Angeles housed both. The famed Musicians Institute of Technology on Hollywood Boulevard was a stone's throw from the Strip and also was home to alumni and faculty, which included members of Mr. Big, David Lee Roth's band, and a number of shredders found in the pages of *Guitar World*. I was also inspired by a fantastic guitarist from North Bay named Paul Quenneville, who had made the journey and studied at GIT, had actually formed a band in Hollywood, and even opened for Lynch Mob! Paul had returned home from GIT and was working at Music City, the local music store. In my eyes, Paul was every bit the conquering hero, and I would hang around Music City for hours soaking up his incredible playing, which incorporated all the techniques he had acquired at GIT, as well as the genuine vibe of someone who had actually "done it." It was the final bit of inspiration I needed to inform my parents that I was moving to Los Angeles to go to GIT!

Of course, GIT came at a pretty steep tuition price (not to mention living expenses!), one that wouldn't necessarily be covered by my income garnered from cutting grass and digging the odd grave at the local cemetery, various bar gigs, and playing guitar in the Pro Cathedral of the Assumption choir. Factor in that I could not find any other musician friends willing to make the same plunge and the understandable reticence of my parents to fund such an endeavour, and I was left looking for other options.

My mother was adamant that all of her children receive a university education, and she was willing to help us make that happen at any cost (savings, the acquisition of student loans, etc.). Well, if university was going to get me to a big city which housed a music scene, perhaps this was something worth looking into!

After a crash course in classical guitar studies (thank you Brian McDowell for prepping an impatient young rocker in the ways of the nylon string!), I was prepared to do entrance auditions for various schools. I set my sights on the University of Ottawa, McGill in Montreal, and the University of Toronto (this was Brian's first choice for me, since he himself had studied with the great Eli Kassner and wished for me to do the same).

Now, in comparison to North Bay, all three of these cities were obviously much bigger, and all three definitely were home to healthy music scenes. But for a young rock devotee enamoured with big hair, loud guitars, and over-the-top anthems, Toronto stood head and shoulders above the pack. I knew this because of a Toronto-based publication distributed nationally through record chains, called *M.E.A.T* magazine (Metal Events Around Toronto). The editor-in-chief, Drew Masters, was a huge champion of the original music scene in Toronto (and ultimately nationally), and he had developed a slick, well-written, and highly inspiring magazine that spoke of local heroes as if they were already stars. It was in these pages that I was regaled with tales of the Yonge Strip scene, and venues like The Gasworks, Rock 'n Roll Heaven (a club in the basement of the The Hudson Bay Centre!), not to mention larger concert venues like RPM and The Spectrum.

Possibly symptomatic of our reliance on the American seal of approval as a culture, it took a nod from America to get *M.E.A.T* magazine up and running in Canada

"I initially went to the U.S. labels to get support for it because I wasn't getting anywhere with the Canadian record companies. [The U.S. labels] said you should go back to the Canadian guys and we'll put in a word for you. I took my own money and I went down to New York and L.A. and hung out with the guys at all the major and minor record labels of the day. They helped me get the buzz going back in Canada, and finally when I got started I got one ad from one label the first time, and then it took off."

Even though *M.E.A.T* started with a very grassroots approach, Masters had his sights on loftier goals. "It didn't start nationally. *M.E.A.T* started locally. Initially it was 20,000 copies in Toronto and then it grew to 35,000 in Southern Ontario, then it grew to 50,000 across Canada, and for a very short period of time I upped it to 100,000, but that wasn't feasible. But you know, at its peak it was 50,000 copies across Canada. It was available in Music World stores. HMV too, plus I had distribution in small independent record stores, clubs, pretty well anybody who had any connection with music."

In fact, it was in one of these small record chain stores, Records on Wheels on Main Street in North Bay, that I would pick up my monthly copy of *M.E.A.T* and read about all of these young musicians making a go of it not only in Toronto, but all across the country. *M.E.A.T* magazine really did bring the nation's hard rock and metal bands together and made it seem possible to break out of one's hometown scene. To me and many other musicians who wanted to write and perform original music on the domestic and world stage, *M.E.A.T* magazine was the inspiration to stop expending energies on covers of songs by our heroes and to start aiming at taking our rightful places on the world's stages and record store shelves right beside them.

"Up until then you were either a tribute band or a cover band and that was it. And you know, I understand that for a smaller community. I get that you're not expected to make it from like Val-d'Or, Quebec, or something, although that's really changed today with the Internet. You can be a good band in the middle of nowhere, put on something on YouTube, and people go 'wow.' If there's enough interest, then you'll get out there. But that didn't exist back then, you had printed press, that was basically it. [You had] *The Power 30* or *The Power Hour* or whatever MuchMusic was doing at the time, and they barely ever played original [independent] bands' videos on there because of the production values, both visually and sound-wise, so the number one medium was print media. And for hard rock and metal, it was *M.E.A.T.*"

Another thing that made *M.E.A.T* such a fascinating read was the fact that it really did make local stars out of bands that might not have had such a polished promotional outlet. Masters and *M.E.A.T* made it possible for bands like Attitude, Succsexx, Jack Damage, Thunder Circus, Nitemare, and a host of other Toronto bands to get credible ink in a magazine directly aimed at fans with a voracious appetite for anything that Drew gave a "horns up" to. One band in particular, Slash Puppet, seemed to have everything going for them. Their shows were literally packed to the rafters, they crafted excellent songs in the dirty street style of the late eighties/early nineties, they had the looks, the swagger ... but somehow the big record deal eluded them, despite securing the management services of SRO, the company that handles Rush. I remember people at the time saying the band was overhyped, but in my eyes they were every bit as deserving as any band who did secure a recording contract.

"Let's just say there was a YouTube back in the day, or the way things are now. I think Slash Puppet would have been monster huge. Monster huge. I think if they had been renamed and repackaged, they could have really been huge. I think they would have been a monster band up there like Killer Dwarfs and stuff, you know? For example, Helix and 'Rock You,' that level of success in the U.S., I think Slash Puppet could have had that with their stuff. I think Slik Toxik should have been bigger with 'Helluvatime.' It also was that these bands were coming off kind of the tail end of an era. We didn't realize at the time that it was; we thought the era was going to go on forever. But little did we know that, you know, there was going to be this big upheaval in music coming from Seattle. I mean, have you ever seen a music genre just dumped en masse by record labels like hard rock was in the mid-nineties?"

Alas, that is talk for another, less inspiring chapter.

It was through *M.E.A.T* magazine that I read about Slik Toxik signing their big U.S. record deal with Capitol. It was also in the pages of *M.E.A.T* where I first noticed that there was indeed a hierarchy of record deal types. According to Masters, not all animals were equal.

"Back when I did *M.E.A.T* nobody wanted the Canadian record deal, everyone wanted to get noticed in the States. If you got a U.S. record deal, that was the holy grail. If it was 'oh we signed to Attic,' it was like 'that's too bad.' I mean, really, it came down to that it almost felt like you were a second-class citizen of rock 'n roll if you got a Canadian record deal, which was really sad because they did have really good connections for distro and stuff. And it didn't hurt bands, it seems, in the seventies. It didn't hurt BTO or April Wine. Why was it not working for Anvil when they signed with Attic in the early eighties? Why didn't it work for other bands going forward from there that signed with the various Canadian labels at the time?"

This is a conundrum faced in all levels of Canadian art and media ... and certainly isn't one I am going to attempt to solve here. You could make a strong argument that Drew Masters did more than his share for pushing forward Canadian metal and hard rock in the late eighties and early nineties with *M.E.A.T* (a task he still undertakes to this day in the digital realm via the *M.E.A.T* magazine Facebook page).

"I think the most important thing that *M.E.A.T* did was open up the door for bands to be original in Canada and actually feel that they were going to get noticed and have a shot. I sent the magazine to every major and indie label, every major label in the States. We had a huge mailing list. And that was on my dime, *my* dime. I sent it by packing each mag in a brown envelope, doing all the stickers and the stamps and sending them out. I mean, I spent considerable money that I could have just pocketed because I put it out to everybody in the States and we did the conventions. We did the Foundations Forum conventions in both New York and Los Angeles. We were in the faces of the Americans. I think we were as important as *Kerrang!* was from England and *Burrn!* from Japan. You know, it meant something."

One of the bands that I was made familiar with thanks to *M.E.A.T*'s efforts was Winter Rose, which housed at one point not one but two of Canada's most successful musical exports, vocalists Sebastian Bach and James Labrie. Rob Laidlaw, currently bassist for Platinum Blonde, is a Toronto musician who has served in a number of bands from the eighties and early nineties. He was the bassist on Lee Aaron's *Some Girls* album, laid the bass down on Helix's *It's a Business Doing Pleasure* record, and also was a member of Gypsy Rose, a Toronto band that inked a deal with KISS icon Gene Simmons' humbly named Simmons Records. Just as a rose by any other name would smell as sweet, Laidlaw has continued to enjoy a busy career thanks to the training afforded him in Toronto's hard rock scene.

"Winter Rose played all the classic spots, Rock 'n Roll Heaven, The Gasworks, Larry's Hideaway, etc. Winter Rose never got a deal, although we had Atlantic Records come up to see us three times. In the end they poached our singers, Baz for Skid Row and James for Dream Theater, then we gave up. I met my wife at the legendary Rock 'n Roll Heaven (when my kids ask where I met Mom, I say Heaven). I have great memories of that time. It was a great scene with great players, lots of chicks, and many laughs."

Stacey Blades from L.A. Guns fondly remembers his days in the scene in Toronto that *M.E.A.T* helped foster.

"Yeah, it was really great. The one cool thing that I remember about the whole scene was that there were lots of great places to play, and I remember towards '89, '90, '91 it was really kind of peaking. I especially remember the summer of '91. It always seemed that Canada was just a little bit behind what was going on in the States, but I remember specifically that summer of '91. I had a band called Fraidy Cat, which was a really good band, and there were just so many other bands. I remember flyering for shows downtown on poles and construction boards for a show at Rock 'n Roll Heaven and maybe an hour later all the posters would be fucking covered up by competing bands! I remember *Metal Edge* magazine, which was the biggest hard rock magazine at that time of the eighties and early nineties doing a whole thing [on the Toronto Scene]. Gerri Miller [*Metal Edge* magazine editor] came down from L.A. and did this whole big article saying that Toronto was the next hard rock city, it was the next L.A., and we all thought, *Okay, this is it, we're finally making some noise here. We're gonna get signed, Toronto is on the map now!* I remember Sven Gali ... you could go to any club [they were playing] and the place would be just packed with chicks. They were rock stars to me, you know?"

Bars like The Gasworks, Rock 'n Roll Heaven, and Larry's Hideaway in Toronto, Hot Rocks in Brampton and Entex in Mississauga were places where the well-heeled (and high-heeled) rocker could go to "party on" in true *Wayne's World* fashion. Having arrived just at the tail end of the hair metal party in that summer of '91, I can attest to the fact that it really was a great time. From my first quart of Molson Export (thank you, fake ID!) to my first big city hair metal hookup (thank you, Sven Gali concert at RPM), Toronto at this time was really the stuff that hair metal dreams were made of. With two of the best hard rock clubs (Rock 'n Roll Heaven and The Gasworks) and two of the best strip clubs (The Brass Rail and The Zanzibar) located on Yonge Street, it truly was our version of the Sunset Strip.

In a beautifully written article that Drew Masters posted on the *M.E.A.T* magazine Facebook page, he perfectly summed up the look and feel of the Toronto scene in his description of Rock 'n Roll Heaven, which, along with The Gasworks, was really the spiritual home of the hair metal scene.

"Heaven," as it was simply known to its legions of loyal patrons, was more than just another rock club; it was "the" social hub for the ever-youthful rock/metal "nation" of Toronto and surrounding area to merge at on a weekly basis and become one in spirit.

With the ever-pounding, guitar-shredding, ear-piercing tones of the mid-eighties/early-nineties hair band music era as the lifestyle's soundtrack, spending time in Heaven — located in the basement of a commercial building at the busy northeast corner of Yonge and Bloor Streets — was both an aural and visual spectacle.

At times it was a challenge — especially to outsiders — to distinguish the girls from the boys, since it was virtually mandatory that all had to possess long (and longer!) hair that both reached for the sky and the floor simultaneously.

Even many of the era's glitzy fashion style choices, often referred to as "glam," were virtually interchangeable. Most memorably, Heaven's flamboyantly attired "styling and profiling" cast of regulars added to the venue's devilish charm and decadent character.

Yet Heaven wasn't always for the "posers"; it also catered, on several select evenings, to those into "speed/thrash" metal, bringing together the more simplified and straightforward denim-and-leather crowd for many memorable nights of beer-guzzling and headbanging.

Even those rock fans with no particular "scene" affiliation would at times dare venture into the club, for the enjoyment of the music/acts, to see what the buzz was all about, or to simply gawk in amazement at the decked-out patrons — especially the oh-so-sexy twenty-something girls, who often were dressed to impress in tight tops, micro-minis, sheer hosiery, and stiletto heels.

And when the era's most famous rock stars were in town, be they here on promotion, on off nights between tour dates, or after-concert performances, they too came to Heaven to "hang." Superstars such as Mötley Crüe's Nikki Sixx and Tommy Lee, Judas Priest's Rob Halford, Toronto's own homegrown sensation Sebastian Bach (then of Skid Row), and many, many others made the trek to Heaven, attracted by its aura and reputation.

And though it thrived (as all clubs essentially do) on its meat-market status, it survived and became legendary because of the music, always delivering the best of the best. Be it an emerging, up-and-coming international hard rock/metal act, a well-known legacy rock act still on the road (yet well past its prime), or a performance by a locally based act consisting of some of the club's peers dreaming and desiring to make it in the music industry, Heaven was Toronto's "must-do" venue above all others.

And despite its many technical inadequacies — the low ceiling height, below-average stage size, reduced sightlines, etc. — not once to my knowledge did anyone refuse to play the venue, since all acts, both local and international, were fully aware that Toronto's Rock 'n Roll Heaven was *the* place in the city, if not Canada, to play and be seen, no matter what the limitations. In fact, the limitations forced many acts to strip away the over-indulgent showbiz glitz of the era and just plain plug in, kick ass, and rock!

The careers of many Canadian musicians/acts, and the Canadian success of many international acts, were a direct result of how they won over, or lost, Heaven's overly judgmental "seen it all" crowd. Encores at Heaven weren't a given, they had to be earned.

Simply put, Heaven was one-of-a-kind: a much loved, all-genre rock/metal mega-club. In today's Toronto club scene, there is nothing else even remotely close to it. Perhaps there never will be again. It is fondly remembered, and sadly missed, by all who knew it as their second home.

Speaking of scenes, it always seemed to me that there was some contention between various subgenres of metal ... purveyors of hair metal would be called "posers" or "glam-fags" by the denim vest–wearing and high-top sneaker–sporting thrash set. Conversely, thrashers were sometimes seen as being a little lower on the evolutionary scale, with slights about hygiene and their lack of ability to draw women to their shows. But when it came right down to it, were they all that different? Was the teasing just good-natured fun, or was there a real sense of disdain between thrashers and glam metal guys? Not in the case of Voivod's Langevin.

"Coney Hatch came to where we came from, up north, a couple of times in the early eighties and the drummer, Dave Ketchum, was a huge influence on my style. I thought they were absolutely great live. Coney Hatch and Anvil, which also came to town, and Anvil had a huge influence on us as well. I watched the drummer, Robb Reiner, a lot and I learned a lot of tricks from him, just watching him. Incidentally, in 2010 we played the Wacken Open Air Festival in Germany. We played with Anvil, and Lips still remembers us sitting front row — because they played for one week [in Jonquière] when they came, and we would be there the whole week, you know? And Lips still remembers us sitting there front row every night. I was always a fan of hard rock and to me hair metal was a continuation of a lot of the stuff I was listening to when I was younger, which was hard rock, Led Zeppelin and such. So I never really had any prejudice, and actually when we were touring in the eighties, every time we would stop in L.A. to play, afterwards we would go to the Sunset Strip because we also played The Whisky and The Roxy. I have really fond memories of those years for sure."

"There were a few musician friends of ours who were in the glam or hard rock scene," says Sacrifice's Rob Urbinati, "but I always got the impression that many of these bands looked down on us. Like the music we played wasn't valid or something. They were all shooting for the huge major label deal and although they were playing bars, they still had to carry themselves with that 'rock star' behaviour. The only redeeming thing for us now is that twenty-five years later, people are still buying our music, still inviting us to play festivals, and those bands for the most part didn't release anything and are forgotten. There was no competition — we were on two totally different sides of the fence. There was camaraderie with some of those bands, though, the ones that could appreciate what we were about or we could watch the guitarists shred and appreciate musicianship."

For the most part, bands of specific subgenres stuck together, playing on bills with other artists in a similar vein.

"We did a lot of early touring with Anvil, but they had been around for years before we burst on the scene," says Mike Campagnolo of Razor. "Also, bands like [Ottawa, Ontario's] Exciter and Voivod were amazing, and bands like Sacrifice and Slaughter did some memorable shows with us, at the defunct Larry's Hideaway in Toronto. Those bands were both awesome examples of the early thrash scene."

Another street in Toronto at the time was also burgeoning with original music. Queen Street was (and is) home to the famed Rivoli club, the Horseshoe Tavern, the Bamboo Club (now gone), and a number of other establishments that hosted music that was, to my mind, the polar opposite of hard rock and metal. It seemed like getting signed to a record deal was almost an *afterthought* to some of these bands ... they didn't dress like the type of rock star I wanted to nor did they sound it. Bands like Cowboy Junkies, Change of Heart, Bourbon Tabernacle Choir, Leslie Spit Treeo, Blue Rodeo (who were already well established as Canada's most successful purveyors of alt-country), The Look People, and some band called Barenaked Ladies were rootsier, more downhome, less assuming looking ... it all just seemed a little plain to me. Of course, as I began to broaden my social horizons at the University of Toronto, I realized that some of my fellow music students were quite active in these "alternative" music scenes ... and they actually had pretty strong negative opinions about the kind of music I liked and the scene I was into. I believe the descriptive terms I heard most were "pedantic," "sexist," "juvenile," and "shitty."

Glen Milchem is a musician who has spent some time on both streets. He first came to my attention as the drummer with Andy Curran, who launched a successful Juno award-winning solo career after his stint with Coney Hatch. Milchem would later go on to join Blue Rodeo, playing a decidedly different type of music. Who better to perhaps illuminate the differences (perceived and actual) between the scenes on the two streets?

"I was parachuted into the early nineties metal scene in Toronto when I joined Andy Curran and Soho 69 in 1990. I'd met Andy the year before when we both played on Malcolm Burn's solo album, which was released on Anthem, the label which had signed Andy's previous band, Coney Hatch. He remembered me when starting his new project and asked me to come out and audition for the recording of Soho 69's first album, which was being produced by Kim Mitchell.

"Prior to that I had been touring and recording with T.O. singer/ songwriter Andrew Cash and playing with various local Toronto bands. Though none of these were metal bands, I'd developed a taste for metal in the late nineties and was a big fan of bands like Motörhead, Metallica, Slayer, and Danzig. For me, it was a natural progression from my fondness for punk bands. Though Andy's music was more in the Aerosmith vein of poppier hard rock, the idea of playing something big, loud, and snotty appealed to me, and I needed a gig. I recorded the album with them and a short while later we started touring.

"The metal scene in Toronto at that time was vastly different from the Queen Street scene I was familiar with. In most Queen Street clubs, people tended to dress down. Roots music was fairly prevalent in the wake of Blue Rodeo's rise to national popularity, and not being flashy or pretentious was the norm. Grunge had yet to take hold in Toronto, so bands were for the most part relatively tame in terms of volume and heaviness. At Rock 'n Roll Heaven and The Gasworks, on the other hand, the epicentres of Toronto hair metal, people were fully decked out in leather, studs, hairspray, and makeup. Over-the-top bands like Slik Toxik were popular, and the clubs were rammed with people wanting to see, be seen, and get laid. The music was disposable but fun, which was exactly what the people who went to those clubs were looking for. Soho 69 mostly played Rock 'n Roll Heaven in Toronto, and it was always a big deal when we did.

"For me, playing with Andy Curran was an eye-opener because it was my first exposure to the whole hair metal milieu of groupies, strip joints, dive bars, and motels. I was already a dad with a five-year-old son and a seven-year-old stepson, and didn't really adapt well to the sleaze factor. Musically it was no problem, because I loved to play hard, loud, and fast (still do). But after a while I started to miss playing music that was a little more dynamic. After a year of touring I left the band. Shortly after that, Nirvana became huge, effectively killing off hair metal and driving the metal scene back underground.

"I went back to playing with Andrew Cash as well as other Queen Street bands like Groovy Religion and Change of Heart, two bands that could be pretty heavy in their own right. Shortly after that I got the gig with Blue Rodeo. In my spare time I've continued to play off and on with a variety of loud bands (e.g. Holy Fuck, my brother's band Starvin' Hungry, Big Sugar), and I still enjoy metal. Musically I'm an opportunivore, I love all flavours and styles."

The sleaze factor that Milchem talks about is an interesting one. In fact, it is what made the hard rock and metal scene tough to swallow for many people who might otherwise have really dug the music. Now, a true, dyed-in-the-wool rocker would probably just scoff at this, call the Queen Street scenesters a bunch of pussies, and get on with his partying. But I have to admit, I never really adapted well to that sleazy scene either. Don't get me wrong, there were plenty of nights spent partying at strip joints and consuming whatever was going around, all in the name of rock 'n roll, but it was always secondary to the music, a complement to the energy of a night enjoying a live concert. But the more time I spent with people who were part of the Queen Street scene, the more I was able to see the absurdity of the behaviour of some of the people on the Yonge Street scene. In fact, it made me a little defensive because I really believed that a band like Slik Toxik had a *lot* more to say both lyrically and musically than some of the so-called music intelligentsia might give them credit for. In my eyes, what I saw in bands like Slik Toxik and Sven Gali was the musicianship, the struggle to get great and über-proficient at their craft, and the desire to entertain. But those qualities were blurred in the eyes of people who, fairly enough, only saw the abusive partying and rampant sexism that was inherently part of the scene that bred these bands. Nick Walsh and Slik Toxik lyricist Dave Mercel might have been warning people about cocaine abuse in a song like "White Lies, Black Truth," but I think a lot of people only saw the strippers in the video and the flowing hairdos. And just as I was enjoying the very peak of the Canadian hard rock scene in Toronto in 1991, my new acquaintances were introducing me to concepts that would make me question the moral and ethical validity of some of the excessive behaviour that had come before me in the scene, behaviour I had taken part in. I may have been looking California, but soon enough I was going to start to feel a bit Minnesota.

METAL QUEENS: CANADA'S FEMALE HARD ROCK PRESENCE

I've been wringing my hands over how to start this chapter. Part of me wants to completely deny the stereotypical role of the female in hard rock and metal in the eighties and early nineties. It's embarrassing to think back on how women have been portrayed in both musical and visual terms. Mötley Crüe put women into cages with torches in their "Looks That Kill" video, forced into subjugation at the hands of their captors (subjugation in this case being the wail of pointy B.C. Rich Guitars, Vince Neil's banshee vocals, and Tommy Lee's monster double bass kit). Germany's Scorpions were notorious for their warped sexuality (album titles like *Virgin Killer* didn't help, and who can forget their suggestion that hungry bitches should be fed with the band's collective "inches" in "Rock You Like a Hurricane"). W.A.S.P. songs like "On Your Knees," "Sex Drive," and "Animal (Fuck Like a Beast)" were raw, graphic, hyper-sexualized anthems aimed squarely at the raging hormones of the fourteen-year-old male consumer. Whitesnake was gonna "slide it in, right to the top" … and they weren't ever gonna stop. And as for the fabled backstage activities of hard rock and metal bands, all one has to do is read *The Dirt*, Mötley Crüe's autobiographical tale of (amongst other things) sexual depravity in the guise of rock 'n roll hijinks.

But as a kid, and really for the most part as an adult, all of this overblown sex stuff didn't really faze me ... well, it probably messed up my perception of proper male-female relationships in a very subliminal yet scarring way. But aside from that, I don't think I ever gave a rat's ass what Ratt was singing about — the words just didn't matter that much to me. I was more into the *sound* of the words, the rhythmic thrust of the syllables and the attack of the consonants. Still, when you actually read these lyrics out loud (as my mother made me do to her just prior to one of our "record smashing" sessions, an event that occurred quite often during the heady days of the PMRC, an American censorship group founded by bored Washington Wives, who made it their mission to save the youth of America from Satan, Tits, and Ass), you can't argue with how vile, sexist, and offensive they can be.

Don't get me wrong here. I fully embrace that rock 'n roll is largely governed by sexuality (the term itself was fifties slang for the act of doin' the nasty). It is a sexual music, but somewhere within the eighties heavy metal paradigm, things got confused. This was not the free love of the Woodstock sixties, and it went beyond the narcissistic mutual sexual exploration of the disco seventies. Sexuality in hard rock and heavy metal seemed to be about power. Men were in control of what seemed from the outside to be a very one-sided sexual power play. It seemed that women were quite content to sprawl over sports cars in videos as they performed scantily clad interpretive dance moves for the lion-maned paramours in the band. The message was pretty clear. The boys played in the band, and the girls played *with* the band, if they were chosen to do so.

Canadian bands didn't seem to flaunt this kind of perspective as loudly as their American counterparts. I mean, Helix did like to have "uncensored" versions of some of the videos for the songs "Gimme Gimme Good Lovin'" and "Rock You" with scantily clad women in various states of undress. And you might catch a Brighton Rock video with a few groupies milling around the band ... but overt sexism wasn't *really* at play in the Canadian scene.

For me, my first connection with women in hard rock was through female-fronted acts. In my earliest musical memories, it was through the work of Vancouver's Headpins (fronted by vocal powerhouse Darby Mills) and the band Toronto, led by vocalist Anne "Holly" Woods and guitarist Sheron Alton. Later on, after already establishing a career in Europe, Lee Aaron became the first name in female Canadian heavy metal.

I'd be lying if I said that the fact that these were beautiful women playing my favourite type of music was lost on me … I was well aware of the power and magnetism of the looks that went with the hooks. But their sexuality wasn't the be-all and end-all for me and the string of gold and platinum records accrued by these acts is testament to the fact that at the end of the day, gender doesn't have any bearing on the quality of the music.

Still, knowing the political climate of the eighties and nineties with regards to gender equality, one has to wonder if being a female musician brought its own unique set of challenges, considering the "Old Boy's Club" mentality that dominated the music industry at that time. I also wanted to know what the similarities and differences were in the pursuit of the rock 'n roll dream when it came to gender.

Being a hard rock pioneer in Canada meant that there wasn't a template in front of you. Was there something about heavy rock that drew in these artists, or were they simply taking the opportunity afforded them to get out and perform?

"No, I never really set out to be in a hard rock band at all," says Lee Aaron. "My background is musical theatre, and I spent most of my years as a youth singing old Broadway standards, Gershwin, Rodgers and Hart, the Tin Pan Alley repertoire. I was spotted singing in a production and asked to audition for a local rock band when I was barely fifteen years old. I was asked to join the band 'Lee Aaron' and the next thing I knew I was singing Led Zeppelin … not that that's a bad thing."

Did Lee experience or notice a difference in the treatment of female hard rock musicians, or a different reaction from audiences due to gender?

"Absolutely. Back then, many male musicians and industry types just dismissed input from a girl. It was a foreign concept in the alpha-male world of hard rock. I had to fight for every scrap of respect in some instances. If you were attractive, it was almost harder, because that era in particular objectified women to the max. Everyone wanted to exploit beauty from a marketing perspective, but when it eclipsed the songwriting and the performance, I found it very difficult. Then you've established an idol-worship scenario with your audience and that is not sustainable. In fact, it's pretty lonely at times, because you cannot possibly live up to people's expectations."

As I was coming up in the clubs, I would sometimes hear disparaging comments from jealous male musicians about successful female musicians, and how they managed to "secure" some of their professional opportunities. My ears told me that this was bullshit, but I always wondered whether the road to rock 'n roll fulfillment was markedly different for a female musician. The public is always hungry for something new and different, so was there a novelty factor attached to these pioneering hard rockers? Was it easier or harder to establish a career in Canada?

"Easier, in that I was one of the first women playing a more aggressive style of rock in Canada, so it merited much attention. It was easy to get noticed. Harder, because Canadian radio wouldn't touch my first four albums, I couldn't get a decent opening slot, and many people thought I was a novelty act. I spent a lot of time touring Europe. That said, I did have a few great supporters in the beginning like Keith Sharp (*Music Express*), Daniel Richler, and J.D. Roberts from MuchMusic's program *The New Music*."

Europe proved to be very receptive to Canadian female hard rock artists. *Classic Rock* magazine's specialty offshoot AOR magazine had Aaron, Woods, and Mills listed in their Top 50 Female Vocalists of all time, with Mills and Woods both finishing in the Top 10. Aaron had her first taste of big time success overseas. Like so many other Canadian artists before, Lee had to go elsewhere to find validation and success as an artist before being accepted as a star in Canada.

Kinda makes you wonder ... was Europe more open to the concept of a female performing hard rock and heavy metal music?

"Yes, I was a breakout star in Europe long before Canada. I had sold over 100,000 records on a small indie label out of Belgium called Roadrunner. I remember returning after touring Europe with Bon Jovi, where I was playing soft-seaters, topping music magazine polls, and being courted by Virgin Records — to driving across Canada with my Attic

Records promo rep almost begging stations to play the new album, and they just weren't interested. In Europe I was made to feel like a great rock artist who happened to be female. In Canada, I was a cute chick singing rock. People didn't even realize I wrote my own songs."

For Darby Mills, the European exposure that the Headpins received did not betray any sort of prejudice against women — in fact, they were welcomed as a support act by one of the most overtly macho bands of the era, England's Whitesnake. Her experience touring abroad ranks as a career highlight.

"In the mid-eighties when the Headpins went overseas, it appeared the audiences were rock 'n roll crazy ... I got the feeling they were just about to explode. Jon Lord, Cozy Powell, John Sykes, and of course, David Coverdale ... the Hammersmith Odeon, the beer, the shopping, the beer, the guards at the airport with the automatic rifles. I was twenty-three years old, what a rush!"

For her part, Holly Woods did not notice any perceivable difference in her career struggles. "Nope, I have personally never noticed any different treatment from anyone because of my gender. My tour experiences are different, of course, but only because I may get a bit lonely being the only 'girl' [laughs]. I *have* always said that Canadian musicians work harder for everything. They also never forget where they came from, no matter how high their star rises."

With all the good humour honed from years on the road with the rock 'n roll boys club, Mills offers this perspective.

"Do I think it made it easier to reach career pursuits? If landing a man was your objective, *yes*! [laughs] I think at that time in the music industry, women were mostly novelties, at least on the rock/metal end of it. Here's the thing, though ... I didn't and don't think of the Headpins as metal. I thought of us as rock, just rock! We were all, no matter what genre, in the same pursuit for air time, so call it what you will as long as it gets played. Back then, you had to have a hook, something to set you apart! As long as someone else had already done it and it was a success [laughs]. I [as a female musician] was partly the hook, as were Ab and Brian because they were from two bands at the same time, even though we were not allowed to mention that at first. They were still under contract with Chilliwack."

For Aaron, inspiration came from a band fronted by two American sisters from Seattle who forged their first successes in Vancouver, a British rock band who threw caution to the wind in its musical diversity, and a jazz singer whose influence would be more readily heard later in Lee's career.

"Heart ... I got the *Dreamboat Annie* album when it came out in 1976 and spent the next fifteen years trying to be half as cool as Ann and Nancy Wilson. Led Zeppelin. They fused metal and folk and blues together into something absolutely transcendent. Nina Simone. She had such a unique gift on piano and singing. No one sounds like her."

Taking inspiration from Tina Turner, Janis Joplin, and Heart, Darby Mills had a deliciously raunchy vocal style that fit perfectly with the roaring guitar riffs of Chilliwack guitarist Brian "Too Loud" McLeod, who discovered Darby after her stints fronting the bands Business Before Pleasure and Steelback.

"I jumped at the opportunity that the Headpins offered me. It gave me the opportunity to work live shows and go on tour. There was no one but male musicians then, and for every guy that had an attitude [about female musicians] there was another one that really liked you [laughs]. For the most part live audiences saw that I was not playing around! I worked hard, very hard on stage. I was committed to the show, and I was as badass as any of the boys ... or at least that's the persona that I think I gave off. Reminding the crew and management that I was *not* one of the guys was futile. I had to change in the toilet all the time. 'An extra change room? What for!' was the attitude."

It should be noted that Too Loud also discovered Canadian belter Chrissie Steele in the Vancouver bar scene at the dawn of the nineties, choosing her first as a replacement for Mills in a new version of the Headpins but ultimately helping her land a deal as a solo artist, due to his fight with cancer, which tragically claimed the Canadian guitar hero's life on April 25, 1992. Her debut album, *Magnet to Steele*, was released on the Chrysalis label and yielded the hit "I'm Gonna Love Ya Till it Hurts."

Did these female artists ever feel pressure from their management, record labels, or bandmates to conform to an image that they did not feel comfortable with?

"Yes, there were times I felt a *lot* of pressure from the industry to conform to a certain image, but I did it my way anyway," says Holly Woods.

Aaron also felt the strain and conflict of image pressures.

"Yes. It was an ongoing battle, yet on an emotional level I felt I had to give some merit to the fact that perhaps I couldn't see myself, imagewise, objectively. Red spandex shorts, however, were definitely a mistake I'd like to live down."

While Mills didn't feel external pressure, she does look back with some levity on some of her wardrobe choices.

"Ha-ha ... no, that is the one thing they left me to fuck up all on my own! I look back on some of the stuff I wore and think, *Oh my God, what were you thinking*? But it was the eighties. What were any of us thinking?"

There are some well-documented early marketing choices involving one of these artists in particular and a certain men's magazine that would make for more titillating reading ... but I can't bring myself to bring it up here, even with the research right in front of me. It quite simply is too easy to define these artists out of the context of their true talent. The difference between crass sexual exploitation and the very pure transfer of sexual identity is marked and crucial to uphold, and these artists transcended the slights and challenges of negative perception by demonstrating undeniable talent and rocking as hard or harder than the boys.

the peaks: grabbing rock 'n roll's brass ring

"I'm going to make it!" is a very simple sentence but a very complex statement. I think that musicians have been striving to get to "it" for a long time, and I am not sure you *can* ever truly get there. If I've learned anything in my own journey as a musician, it is that a huge part of the rush of pursuing the rock 'n roll dream is found in the striving — the carrot of accomplishment of an objective or goal that is dangled in front of us. What is wonderful about the life of a musician is that our ambitions are *not* blind, but rather they are in the name of something we truly love: our art and our music. When you take into consideration the struggles and hardships of most musicians who choose this career path, it is pretty hard to deny that it is done for any reason than love and passion.

But that is not to say there is not incredible satisfaction in achieving the markers of success that can be found (albeit not by many) along the journey. The first record deal, the first sold-out club show, the first packed stadium performance, or that first gold or platinum album, the first piece of free gear from an endorsement ... this is the stuff dreams are made of, those moments that shock and electrify the system. But the moments are fleeting, and anyone who has known success as a musician knows that we are sharks in the water. We need to keep moving to stay alive.

These artists are my heroes. I looked up to them and spent a fair amount of time wondering how it must have felt to achieve the levels of success they did. I wanted to *feel* how they felt in front of that arena crowd or when they were receiving those gold and platinum awards. What are the moments that stand out in the memory of these artists? What are the absolute highlights of a life dedicated to rock?

Lee Aaron: "Getting my first gold record award in Canada meant something. Having [Rush manager] Ray Danniels call to thank me personally for creating a hard rock category at the Junos so Rush finally received one … that meant more than actually winning a Juno. Playing a concert on Mt. Kitzeinhorn in the Austrian Alps was mind-blowing to me when I was twenty-three. I realize that some of these things are more special memories than highlights. I don't really equate them with effort."

Andy Frank, Sven Gali: "Sven Gali won Heavy Metal Video of the Year at the MuchMusic awards in 1992. That year we had two Juno nominations, we did a live concert for MuchMusic on a mountain at Whistler, festivals with Def Leppard that summer. Speaking very personally, I don't remember ever kind of sitting down and taking stock. I just kind of moved on."

Doug Weir, Syre: "For me I think it was the first time I heard one of our songs on the radio. We were driving down the [Highway] 401 together on the way to a gig. It felt great."

Russ Dwarf, Killer Dwarfs: "I think for me it was doing the song 'It Doesn't Matter' [from the *Dirty Weapons* album]. Actually recording that song was just one of those magical days. We did a couple of records with [renowned producer] Andy Johns. The whole experience of working with him on those records was awesome because we grew up listening to all the records that he and his brother [Glyn Johns] did. The guys played so amazing on that record and everybody worked really hard. I've always said that doing records is like a postcard. It's just incredible that we had that kind of experience, and I knew that at the time, too. I just thought you might as well go completely nuts because this may never happen again. For God's sake, we had [Rolling Stones pianist] Nicky Hopkins play on that record!"

Gerry McGhee, Brighton Rock: "I guess getting our first gold record. That was cool. We were doing a show at Canada's Wonderland [a popular Ontario amusement park], we were headlining, and we toured our backs off on *Take a Deep Breath*. We were really burned by the end of that tour. Some places we did three shows in a day and we did everything to push that thing through gold. It went gold and then it climbed real close to platinum too and that was the accumulation of probably five years of non-stop living, breathing, and eating the band and the songs. I mean, we were more married to each other than we were to our spouses at that point because we spent so much time together, so much in the planning and we really were, you know, like brothers. That was probably the peak of everything, where we felt like we began to conquer the world. It was our first step up. We felt good about our songs on the record, we felt good about the fact that it was selling and people seemed to like what we were doing, which was always the biggest buzz. I think we were almost like a gang at that point. It was really the five of us and our crew and we were just kicking ass and taking names later."

Harry Hess, Harem Scarem: "The sheer shock of showing up in Japan and playing a 2,000-seater, and it was jam-packed, like you could not fit another person in there. It was just mind-boggling, travelling across the world, coming out of your dressing room, getting onstage, and looking down and it's full of Japanese people and they're singing along to every song. And you're like 'What the hell is going on?' It was just bizarre. I would say that was the most crazy, fun thing that ever happened to us and I think I speak for everybody in the band because we kind of looked at each other as it was happening in the first song and we were like, 'What the fuck is this?' We had no idea, did not know what to expect. That was a pretty big highlight."

Lips, Anvil: "How about performing for 80,000 people with AC/DC at Magnetic Hill in Moncton, New Brunswick? The biggest show I've ever done in my life. Imagine you've been making your whole career work from outside your country, and then you end up doing the biggest show in your life in Canada? It's like, huh? [laughs] That's a real special one."

Nick Walsh, Slik Toxik: "I don't have any one defining moment, as there were so many childhood goals and dreams fulfilled. I guess when getting some of your childhood heroes coming out to see you perform and then hang with you after as an equal would be considered a career highlight."

Carl Dixon, Coney Hatch: "In general, the Iron Maiden tour represented a high water mark for us in terms of feeling like we belonged there. We were on MTV with our videos and we were on a happening tour and we were making friends with the big guys that we were on tour with, and really learning the ropes of what a band has to do. That meant a lot, that was a confidence that has stayed with me ever since."

Victor Langen, Kick Axe: "Kick Axe went coast-to-coast in the U.S. as opening act several times in succession promoting the *Vices* album. We toured with Judas Priest, Scorpions, Quiet Riot, Ratt, Whitesnake, and Night Ranger. The biggest highlight was having all of Judas Priest come out to see us play after their show at the Calgary Saddledome and having Rob Halford come into our dressing room afterwards to tell us that Great White was fired from the tour and that Kick Axe would now be taking over [the support slot] starting in Madison Square Garden in New York City!"

Daryl Gray, Helix: "One highlight definitely was playing the Spectrum in Philadelphia with Aerosmith. Another was playing the Capital Center in Washington with Rush. We got an encore, and Rush let us take it. Playing the CNE with Scorpions to 26,000 people was definitely a blast."

Michel "Away" Langevin, Voivod: "I think the tour with Rush in 1990. 'Astronomy Domine' was playing a lot on MTV and MuchMusic and here in Quebec on MusiquePlus, and we were asked by Rush to do the eastern leg of their tour in 1990. They were a huge influence on Voivod, and of course Neil Peart was also writing sci-fi concepts, and I really was influenced by him and his drumming as well. They were super nice and super classy people and we were a bit speechless when we met them. A meeting was arranged at the last show by our respective managements, and we didn't say much [laughs]. We were very silent because it was Rush, you know? But they were really nice. Good souvenir."

Derry Grehan, Honeymoon Suite: "One of the highlights would be headlining Maple Leaf Gardens [in Toronto]. And when we used to play Kingswood Music Theatre, that was a fantastic gig because it was the middle of summer — we were on top of the world. We'd go up there and play for two nights. And of course, the first gold record ... that, I still have on my wall. I mean, you're saying 'Wow, we sold fifty thousand records?' And that's nothing in the States, but at that time that was a big accomplishment, so the first one that you get is always kind of the coolest one. We won a Juno, one Juno, but that was still a big deal. Stuff like that you remember forever. And in the States, just being out there touring and playing these huge hockey arenas, where the Red Wings would play the Flyers. All these teams have been playing in these buildings and now you're playing there."

Brian Vollmer, Helix: "I remember on a tour with Triumph jogging around the top of the Montreal Forum, one of hockey's greatest shrines. And playing Maple Leaf Gardens with Kim Mitchell. I remember walking out onstage thinking all the time I was kid that I wanted to play here ... but not in a band, as a hockey player [laughs]."

Sean Kilbride, Haywire: "The one highlight that always sticks out for me was our first big headlining show at the Ontario Place Forum, the home of the revolving stage. We had opened up for Cats Can Fly there a year earlier, but this time it was ours. I was worried. Could we cut it in the big city? Well, we sure did. It was a magical summer night and I couldn't believe that 6,000 people showed up."

Mike Campagnolo, Razor: "For me it was riding the buzz in the early years and watching all your hard work grow into opening for Motörhead, Slayer, and Venom. Every time you hit the stage and hear the roar of approval from die-hard fans, and to still do it years later and get the same rush you felt twenty years earlier all over again, that does it for me."

Rob Urbinati, Sacrifice: "Touring Canada with Razor, playing the No Speed Limit festival in Montreal, finally playing Europe in 2011, all our studio experiences, playing in Japan in 2012 ... but the biggest thing for me was probably our reunion show at the Opera House in Toronto in 2006. We didn't know what to expect after so much time away, but it was an incredible show."

Holly Woods, Toronto: "When I received the All Star Band Techniques Award for best female vocalist in 1982. It was a fan vote-in so it meant the world to me and still does."

For every brief moment of glory and acclaim, there are countless hours of sweat and sacrifice that went into making them happen. The dreams that these musicians chased often came at the expense of comfort and close relationships, even relationships with their own families. I know when I look back on my choices in this pursuit, I mourn for many of those missed summers at the family cottage, the family reunions and birthday parties that I wasn't there for ... I missed out on a lot of wonderful memories. But in reality, it's not only that I wouldn't change a thing, I really *couldn't* have changed a thing. My drive to make music and chase that rush and those fleeting moments really never felt like a choice. It is a vocation, and even in the times when logic tried to pull me out of this career, passion ended up pulling me right back in.

Is the hard work and sacrifice that goes into making a successful career ultimately worth the moments of glory? And were these artists even conscious of the fact they were enjoying the peaks of their popularity as they were experiencing them?

Sean Kilbride, Haywire: "When you're at Budokan in Tokyo and standing on the same stage where Bob Dylan and Cheap Trick recorded live albums, how can you not believe that the work and sacrifice has been worth it? Regretfully, I think back from time to time and realize that I should have lived in the moment more than I did. When we do gigs now, I make sure that I'm paying complete attention to what a privilege it is to still be doing this."

Derry Grehan, Honeymoon Suite: "Hell, yeah, it sure was worth it ... are you kidding me? I mean, you have to remember where you're coming from. Do you want to go back to the bars? No. You're like twenty-four, twenty-five years old, you're not getting any younger. This is your shot and you really may only ever get one, so don't blow it. Yeah, we did enjoy our success ... even with all the work, we were having such a good time, just taking it all in. You have to remember it was the early eighties, and it was a party, you know?"

Daryl Gray, Helix: "Music is what I've always wanted to do, from my earliest memories. The travelling has always been something I've wanted to do, I've been a globetrotter from when I was born ... I love entertaining people so it's always been my goal to do this and to continue to do this as long as humanly possible, so any of the hardships, well, yeah, there's been times when we toured Europe, with Ian Gillan in 1990, and Gillan's pulling up in these two nice big tour buses and we've got like eight guys sleeping in a van with all the gear. I had my spot picked out on the floor. The band has had gold and platinum albums in Canada at this point and been nominated for Juno Awards and here we are, we're still sleeping on the floor in a van because it's something that we needed to do. Did we take time to enjoy our success? It went by very fast. Those heyday years, from maybe '84 to '90–'91 were just a blur because we always were doing something."

Carl Dixon, Coney Hatch: "I don't know if you look at it that way. I think that you're either a lifer or not. What the highlights do is represent a milestone on the road to propel you on to the next thing a little more happily, with a little more juice."

Lips, Anvil: "I would say that [the highlights] were satisfying enough. Quite frankly, if it ended tomorrow I'd think I've gotten everything I've ever wanted out of it ... I have [enjoyed the successes], but it hasn't been easy. There have been people around me that made me feel not good, or tried to make the good feelings not as good as they were ... but I managed to fight through the negativity to enjoy it."

Harry Hess, Harem Scarem: "For me, the real payoff was finishing records. It was writing songs, finishing records. We ended up putting out thirty-six or thirty-eight pieces, and that includes B-sides and singles and all that stuff, so really the satisfaction for me personally was writing songs and being in the studio, because I had my own studio and I was building it up at the time. It was always the focus for me and really why I was doing this. I like being onstage and I like playing but I hated the travel, I hated the wasted time, and it was never something that I overly looked forward to. I looked forward to travelling to other countries I had never been to before and it was almost like 'I'm being paid for this vacation and I'm going to get onstage and play for a bunch of people that really want to see this, and I'm playing my songs,' so it wasn't the same motivation I think a lot of other bands have. For me it was almost like a crazy-weird vacation where music was intertwined with the whole reason I was there, but I just liked making records and writing songs and the rest had to happen because it just had to happen."

Gerry McGhee, Brighton Rock: "Yeah, it was a buzz. I think what made it so much fun was the fact that we were so tight. We really felt like nobody could be replaced at that point in time. During the high times, man, they were pretty special."

Russ Dwarf, Killer Dwarfs: "The bottom line is that you do it because you love music, man. If you're lucky enough to have all that other crap come along, bonus. That's the gravy and everything. How many people are sitting in their basements with the wickedest song that we'll never hear? I'm sure there's a million. We were the lucky ones, man. I'm grateful for my whole career, for whatever has happened to me, completely grateful."

Doug Weir, Syre: "Yes, the whole experience was fantastic. In hindsight I wouldn't give up anything, even the starvation. I might change the odd mistake we made. Absolutely [we enjoyed it], it was like being in a movie. Everything was bigger and crazier than it could have been in the regular world."

Rob Urbinati, Sacrifice: "There are so many memories, great, good, and bad, but we didn't really consider it hard work even though it was … we always loved to write, rehearse, record, and play live. I wouldn't trade my experiences for anything. Not many bands get to experience what we have, and Sacrifice has never even tasted fortune and fame."

Mike Campagnolo, Razor: "Was it worth it? Ask me when I get off-stage next time, you'll get a big thumbs up from me every time!"

Mike Hall, Killer Dwarfs: "Personally, I had a series of small goals I wanted to accomplish with the band. Write good songs, play good gigs, get a big record deal, make records, make videos, meet girls, party all around the world, hang out with cool rock star dudes, and tour the Earth …. and last but not least, maybe make some money at it! We all wished we sold more records, got more airplay, got bigger tours, had a better business plan. But seriously, it was a great time and we had it going on for real! I have no regrets, it was a helluva ride!"

It is pretty remarkable how few musicians I talked to counted financial and material gain as part of their "success." I mean, what other profession puts so much emphasis on the experiences it provides and so little on the remuneration? And isn't that when life is at its most fulfilling? When the task at hand is its own reward? Then again, it doesn't hurt when the industry is throwing massive dollars at you to fuel these experiences (even if not much of it is going in your pocket) and keep them growing bigger and wilder than you could have thought possible.

Yes, when you are the darling of the biz and the kids are gobbling up your records and T-shirts en masse, and your band is managing to fill the seats of the local arena or theatre, it feels like it will never end. And yet this business is a cyclical one. The beginning of the nineties saw metal reaching its commercial apex. It was the soundtrack of youth, the perfect musical complement to sex, drugs, pizza, and whatever the hell else the kids were getting up to. But when that cycle came around for the next big sound, it was stunning to see how quickly and harshly the tables could turn for our hard rock and heavy metal heroes. To paraphrase April Wine's Myles Goodwyn, you have to wonder if anyone ever told the boys (and girls) that rock 'n roll was a vicious game.

the valleys: the gods' descent

At the dawn of the nineties, I truly felt on top of the world. I had moved to Canada's biggest city to pursue my rock 'n roll dream. I was studying classical guitar at a prestigious school. I had managed to find some good-looking, long-haired rock 'n rollers to form a band. We were playing the major venues in town, and we had even managed to secure a manager and have a member of a famous rock band (Jamie Stewart from The Cult) produce our demo. Sure, metal and hard rock as I had known it was changing … it was evolving. Guns N' Roses' *Appetite for Destruction* had started an international trend away from the ultra-refined hair metal sounds and looks of the Sunset Strip. Music was getting tougher, leaner, more street. In my eyes, this was reflected in the music I was hearing from Slik Toxik, Sven Gali, Slash Puppet, and Killer Dwarfs. They were making music that to my ears reflected these principles and they were out there killing it in on the Toronto scene. The fact that bands like Soundgarden, Mother Love Bone, and Alice in Chains were coming out with a thematically and musically darker version of

hard rock and metal was not something that scared me in the least …
in fact, I was embracing these Seattle sounds, along with the sounds of
bands like L.A.'s Jane's Addiction, as the next wave of the music I loved,
not the death knell for the music I believed in and cherished. However,
if I am being honest, there was one band that both thrilled me and terri-
fied me. That band was Nirvana.

Nirvana, not unlike Elvis or The Beatles, is one of those bands that
most people remember hearing for the first time. They remember the
time, the place, and how the music made them feel. I'm no different.

I was at the Faculty of Music at the university when the lead singer
of my band Obscured slipped the headphones of his portable CD player
onto my ears. It was then that I first heard the famous intro to "Smells
Like Teen Spirit," that clean four-chord guitar figure not unlike something you might hear on a Boston record on FM radio, but so, so different. When Grohl launched into his kick and flammed snare intro to
the song's crushingly heavy full-band entry, I was not only floored, but
I also felt something very strange. It was doubt, and doubt that oddly
manifested itself in the realization that the cowboy boots I was wearing,
boots that I had so lovingly adorned with dressings and buckles, were
no longer cool. The bandana that I had so carefully learned to wrap
around my head so that my curly long locks would spill out was soon
going to be a target of derision. It was upon hearing this amazing piece
of music that I realized other people around me were already changing
their look and their attitude. I was late to this party. And I don't think I
was welcome anyway.

Of course, as the nineties progressed, I found myself very lost …
clubs like Rock 'n Roll Heaven and The Gasworks were closing down,
bands that I admired like Slik Toxik and Sven Gali were being panned
not only for attempts at change but for ever existing in the first place. I
personally spent a lot of time trying hard to find my way in a very new
reality, one in which my hopes and dreams were lame and unsure. With
Nirvana came a great cleansing of the sins of overindulgence, stupidity,
and rampant sexism that unfortunately informed a lot of heavy metal
and hard rock. On a musical level, grunge also levelled the boom on the
heavier, more virtuosic forms of heavy music like thrash. Technical proficiency on an instrument was deemed to be baroque and wasteful, and

in much the same way that punk music came along to kill the progressive rock "dinosaurs," so too did it feel like grunge was doing the same with my beloved heavy metal. And I was pissed. Here, I had just begun my musical journey, finally learning the ropes in the clubs, getting my look and sound together … and it all seemed to be going away. My band eventually broke up and I stumbled my way through Toronto's music scene like a stranger in a strange land.

Now, if I felt that way as someone who had yet to achieve a recording contract, had my videos on heavy rotation on MuchMusic, or been on a major tour, how did it feel for the people who had reached some level of success?

Nick Walsh, Slik Toxik: "It was brutal, actually. I mean, to go from thinking that you had a career to wondering how you're even going to present yourself … it was a very, very confusing time. It was one of those things where you just felt like a dog kicked to the curb. And you know, in all facets. It wasn't just like, 'Okay, we're not with this label anymore but our team still believes in us.' It was like we had a manager who was more obviously interested in advance monies and flavours of the week rather than in creating careers. It's like the same old thing, once you do something once and you know how to do it then that becomes the focus. So getting a band and getting a record deal and a big lump sum of money seemed to be the focus from our team at that point. And we, again, being one of the bands that helped them learn the ropes, were sort of cast aside for other possibilities of do-re-me."

Helix experienced a loss that far outweighed any decline in the band's popularity or fortunes. Earlier in this book we heard of the potential dangers of a band touring the rugged terrain of Canada. For most, this is an experience fraught with danger, but one that is ultimately successful and free of tragedy. In a story taken from the Planet Helix website, Brian Vollmer describes the band's darkest day, July 5th, 1992. This was the day Helix lost guitarist and songwriter Paul Hackman.

"The last day of the tour was in Vancouver, British Columbia. The band had the choice of spending $120 for a flight home or riding home in the van for three days. Paul chose to ride in the van and Daryl went along as well because he was taking care of our road management at the time and had paperwork to do. After the show those who were flying went back to the hotel to party and the van left for the U.S. border, since it was a much shorter trip to drive through the States.

"When they arrived at the border U.S. immigration wouldn't let them cross because they didn't have a carnet for the gear, so they were forced to turn around and drive through Canada. About 7:00 a.m., when they were around 60 miles outside of Kamloops, the driver fell asleep and the van left the road, plunging 40 feet down an embankment. The van rolled several times and everyone except Daryl, who was in the passenger seat, was thrown from the van. Daryl told me that when he awoke he was upside down and had to undo his seat belt to get out. He was bleeding badly from numerous cuts he had endured but he managed to crawl up the side of the hill to the main highway.

"All of the guys were lying around on the ground. Some were unconscious, and Paul was moaning and complaining that his chest hurt. Daryl went up to the highway and many cars passed him before a doctor and his wife finally stopped and phoned for an ambulance. Paul died en route to the hospital, probably from internal injuries.

"Back at the hotel in Vancouver, I had gotten up and gone to a writer's place to check out his studio. When I returned, everyone was crying. I immediately knew something was wrong when I walked into the lobby. When they told me Paul was dead, I just couldn't believe it. Of all the people that I knew I thought Paul would live to be a hundred. By that night we were back home and the news was on the radio and TV everywhere. My phone was ringing off the hook but I just ignored it. The next days were spent being hounded by the press. I never knew that they could be so intrusive and rude.

"Hackman was a main component of the songwriting process in Helix, and his tragic end meant not only the loss of a dear friend, but of a powerful musical force. This loss, coupled with the changing tides of taste in the music industry, signalled an accelerated descent into dark days for Helix, and in turn a blow to their identity as a band, and as individuals."

Vollmer goes on to describe the aftermath: "Well you know, aside from Paul dying, which was obviously the lowest of the low, when you're in the public eye and everybody wants to be your friend and then suddenly nobody wants to be your friend — plus, we were going through, as men, mid-life crises. We had all these women, we had all this fucking stuff and then all of a sudden we got into our late thirties or late forties and music was changing, the phone wasn't ringing, and I think that is very hard for a lot of artists to take. Let's face it, we've all got big egos. If you can survive that, it's probably the true test of an artist, that and longevity. Each time you go through a wave of that there's more people who drop out."

At one point you, Vollmer, had gone from an arena-headlining artist to working at a convenience store in your hometown in order to make the rent. Did you look at that as something to be ashamed of?

"Well, it wasn't necessarily something to be ashamed of, but it wasn't anything to be proud of either [laughs]. I've never understood the mentality of people who are proud of being poor. I definitely wasn't proud of being poor. I think I was definitely afraid I was going to die like that, which was a terrible feeling that made me depressed. It probably fortified my faith as a Christian."

An obvious signifier of the decline of popularity of hard rock and metal during this time was the lack of video play the bands were receiving. It was becoming harder and harder to find these acts on TV. I asked former MuchMusic VJ and music programmer Craig Halket if there was a calculated decision to move away from playing heavy metal and hard rock videos in the early to mid-nineties, and if so, what were the determining factors in this decision?

"I think there were a number of factors. One of them was that ratings had started to drop. I think that was more an overall thing. Trends were already starting to change in the early nineties away from people watching music on TV as much as they used to. Certainly there wasn't the Internet, which hadn't really exploded at that point, but viewership numbers were down. When grunge exploded, there was a lot of crossover there, like Alice in Chains, Soundgarden; some would call them hard rock/metal bands but because they were from Seattle, they became grunge bands. Those bands became more mainstream, but they had started on *The Power Hour*. We were playing Alice in Chains and

Soundgarden in the early days and they became more mainstream. So when that happened, there was less requirement for a niche program, and that's when it went from *The Power Hour* to *The Power 30*, and there weren't as many great videos. Certainly a lot of [metal] bands had been around for a long time. There were still those bands, but there was a lot of sameness developing in the early nineties. You know, if you had long hair and you happened to spend some time on the Sunset Strip, it became a little bit clichéd."

Aside from the fall from financial grace and the loss of the adulation and adoration of an adoring fanbase whose tastes have changed, there are other emotional and psychological factors that come from having to face the reality that the endeavour you have poured your heart and soul into is no longer working. When there were bills to pay and mouths to be fed, the deep sense of camaraderie forged by years of digging in the heavy metal trenches was put to a test that sometimes cannot be withstood.

Brighton Rocks' Gerry McGhee elaborates. "I mean, the reality that it's coming to an end is hard. At that point I think we'd probably been together eight or nine years. Around '91 we did *Love Machine*. I think we got together in '83 because I got married in '84. Actually, I got married on the Saturday, and the Monday we were playing in Montreal. I didn't get a honeymoon, but I mean, that was the way it was, that was the way Brighton did things ... I think it may have been a little easier for me because I was the only guy in the band who was married and had kids, so when I used to come off tour, you know, I didn't get the luxury of going to the strip clubs like the rest of the guys, I got put into reality — the garbage needs taking out. A mortgage, you know? Feeding kids. So I always felt I was pretty well grounded, but it was tough when you live and breathe and eat something like that for that amount of time and then all of a sudden you aren't there anymore.

"I guess I would compare it with what an athlete must feel like when he finally retires. When you go through all that stuff and you know your career is over and you are used to the training camps, the playing, flying with the guys, dinner with the guys, sleeping in the dorms with the guys, and then it's done and you are out of the public eye as well. You're not in that arena with TV interviews, radio interviews, the shows, it's all kind of gone and it's a bit of a withdrawal. That's mainly why, after that, I mean, I did spend some time in L.A. after I'd left. I was only thirty years old, but I just said I'm done. I'm officially calling it quits. And I didn't do any more recording, I didn't do any more writing, I just basically closed that chapter of my life and said okay, what am I going to do now? And I'd like to stay in the music industry. Fortunately, I did find my way back in to another end of it. When you've done something for so long and basically been on the road since you were, like, fifteen years old … it was almost half my life and then you come down and say okay, so what do I do to earn a living?"

When the audiences dissipate and the records are no longer selling, there is still one revenue stream that exists beyond a band's commercial peak, provided said band had enough hits that have reached the "classic rock" level of consistent radio airplay. And if you were lucky enough to be one of the writers of the hits, the royalties accrued through music publishing could be enough to sustain the writer through lean times.

Fortunately for Derry Grehan, he was one of those writers and was able to continue to make a living as a musician without having to take another job.

"There's definitely been some valleys over the twenty-five or thirty years, there's been some ups and downs and some really lean times, as you know, being a musician, especially in Canada … being a songwriter, the blessing is the royalties, even though they would be not as much in some periods as they are in others, but I can say, 'Thank God for SOCAN [The Society of Composers, Authors and Music Publishers of Canada, which distributes royalties],' you know? Those things keep you going in real lean times, but we would always try to play a few gigs, even at the lowest point, so I tried not to have to just give it all up and go get a day job. I did anything I could to stay in the music."

For Rick Hughes of Sword, the change from rocking arenas with Bon Jovi to being shoved away into the rock's proverbial "Where Are They Now" files to make way for the new grunge movement was swift and vicious.

"It was like a bushfire, it was finished. No more hair metal, no more heavy metal, no more rock metal ... it was grunge. And the thing is that if you had been a metal player and a metal singer then you could not fake it, even if you tried putting on a different shirt. We were so used to going onstage [with the] rock star attitude and pushing it, and then it all became anti-rock star. Some people tried at the time, I remember. They went from hair metal to grunge, and they changed their clothes but people went 'Nah, I'm not buying it ... you're not gloom, I can feel it, there is happiness in you.' [laughs]"

The hair, makeup, and clothes sported by many hard rock and metal bands seemed to be the focus of a large part of the ridicule hurled at these bands by the rising "anti-rock-star elite." It seemed that the larger-than-life aspects of the heavy metal wardrobe and performance ethic were under attack by a new aesthetic that spat in the flashy faces of eighties-influenced hard rockers. But hey, is laughing at the fashion sense of what came before you really anything new? Did rockers not mercilessly heckle the fashion choices of the disco-loving Studio 54 set? Perhaps it's harder to take when the jokes are coming at your expense, and the jokes came fast and furious to those who had dared to walk as one of the big-haired lipstick-and-leather pack at some point in their careers.

Walsh: "When I was growing up — I've got two brothers ten years older than me, so in the seventies I was, as a kid the same age as my son, six or seven years old, listening to groups like KISS, BTO, Nazareth, Aerosmith, Queen, Alice Cooper, and the list goes on. I was hearing this because it was what my brothers were listening to. That was the seventies and they all wore tight jeans with bell bottoms and, you know, moustaches and long hair [laughs]. That whole bit. And then the eighties came and with the excess that was going on, and I guess the advent of technology and Silicon Valley and all that stuff, then you had bands like Van Halen coming out, all these bands that were a little less dark. They weren't influenced by, let's say, the New Wave of British Heavy Metal, like the Iron Maidens and stuff, which I might add adopted a little bit of that glam look with some of the T-shirts and sweatbands and spandex they wore, but with that excess all of a sudden came guys like David Lee Roth who were more flamboyant. It's kind of like the 'ginos' and 'ginas' in high school with the giant cobra hairdos who drove the Camaro IROCs. When they look back at their school pictures they have a laugh now, too.

"But the thing about grunge coming in was it was the era of the 'anti-rock star.' So if you had hair that was as high as the ceiling, it would now be as low as the ground. It was the complete opposite. And with that came also not just the image but even the music, where it wasn't cool to be able to play anymore. I remember seeing the band Nitro with Jim Gillette and Michael Angelo Batio, these great musicians, technically amazing, but the most over-the-top dress and hair and everything as well. But that was the era, it was flamboyant and part of showmanship. When I go to the circus, I don't want to see the ringleader standing there in a checkered lumber coat going, 'Hey welcome to the show.' And I'm like, 'When did they pull Joe Blow out of the audience and give him the opportunity to be the emcee of the night?' You know what I mean? We're going to see a show. These people are there to entertain us, whether it be with dress, lights, smoke, action, whatever."

One of the Canadian bands that took a lot of flak for a perceived change in their musical approach in the face of the grunge movement was Sven Gali. Their 1995 album *In Wire* was recorded in Seattle by producer Kelly Gray, who had just produced the multi-platinum debut from Candlebox, the archetypal example of "commercial grunge."

Andy Frank: "Yeah. *In Wire* was in lots of ways very different. Somewhere between our first record and *In Wire* it was like the whole music industry flipped on its head. Nirvana and Pearl Jam broke and then there was a huge backlash against eighties rock music, and we were at the end of that wave. So part of that was that we also listened to music and our musical tastes had changed. The actual music that went into *In Wire* was a very natural, organic writing and recording process. It wasn't a grunge record at all ... it was just a very pure creative process, really."

Nick Walsh remembers that, amongst certain members of the rock community back in Toronto, Sven Gali's decision to go to Seattle and record with a "grunge" producer was seen in a different light.

"When Sven Gali did that second record, they went to Seattle and recorded with Kelly Gray. They were in *Seattle,* dude. That was the mecca of the music that killed it for everybody, and they went and did their record there. I mean, for some at that time, they considered Sven Gali traitors!"

But Walsh had been there, too, and is quick to sympathize with the plight of a band that, after making a successful debut album doing the type of music the members loved, now found itself faced with a shift in music industry and popular taste. And herein lies a question: When is a change in direction considered growth, and when is it considered bandwagon-jumping? It seems that the labels sometimes added to the artistic confusion faced by these artists.

"When you're in an industry that's dog-eat-dog and you're striving to survive and make a career out of it and people are telling you what to do, sometimes it gets really confusing, you know? And it's always the band's second album, because when your band signs a deal you think 'This is great, this label believes in us, they believe in our music, our look, our attitude, our live show. They're signing us for *us*, this is fantastic.' You put out the first record, then the second record comes along and now they're telling you what you need to do in order to stay on their label, basically. I remember when we were doing our second record with EMI before we left the label and we were doing demos and stuff. They were telling me, 'Don't scream anymore, that's not happening. Rock screams aren't happening anymore.' The key words were, 'Try to be more organic.' And I'm like, 'We're not Nine Inch Nails! We use real guitars and my voice, how much more organic can you be?' Like, what are you talking about, more organic? Do you mean, dress like Blind Melon and don't bathe for two weeks? Is that more organic? Don't use deodorant? What do you mean? But that was what they were telling us. And meanwhile, at the time they're telling me not to scream, but then you've got a guy like Chris Cornell screaming 'Jesus Christ Pose' and 'Outshined' and stuff. It's like, how much are you really focusing on this music?"

An event that has been widely acknowledged in the Canadian industry as a metaphor for the changing of the musical guard in the early nineties is the infamous "crashed limo incident" at the 1994 Juno Awards. The

174 • Metal on Ice

incident involved Slik Toxik bassist Pat Howarth and has long been a
source of laughs and bad jokes at the expense of Slik Toxik as a band and
metal as a genre. Here, Nick Walsh offers a first-hand account of what
really happened that night.

"We were working with [producer] Glen Robinson and things
seemed to be going rather well, but unfortunately at that time, our
bass player, Pat, was going through some — I guess you could call
it a depression — he had a disability that everyone was pretty much
unaware of at the time, because you know when you're partying all the
time and self-medicating with alcohol and legal narcotics and so forth,
you know it's really, really easy to mask what's really going on. Unfortunately, he was going through something and he was taking a certain
kind of medication that didn't really — what's the word, the cocktail of
the medication and alcohol didn't really sit well and he wasn't himself.

"He happened to get walked out to a limousine that unfortunately
was running. All the limousines outside of this big Capitol-EMI Juno
party were running, much like tour buses. So you know, we had already
taken out our guitar player, Rob, who had said, 'I've had too much to
drink, I don't want to make an ass out of myself. I'm going to go into limo
and just sleep this off until it's time to go.'

"So next on the list was Pat. We walked him out and thought everything was going to be okay. Five or ten minutes later I got a tap on my
shoulder. Somebody who worked at the place asked me if I was the singer
of Slik Toxik. And here I am, thinking, *Hey dude, you want my autograph?* [laughs] He says, 'The two gentlemen that you just walked out
to the car? Well, they've just written it off up the street.' And that was
the beginning of the end, so to speak. Again, the odd part about this
story is, first of all, here's a guy going through some personal troubles.
Nobody's concerned about that. Everybody's more concerned with the
negative press it's gonna bring. And let's sweep it under the carpet. If this
was the U.S., they would have made sure we had a single to release a week
later and that everybody and their mother put us on the front page of the
magazines [laughs]. You know, that would have made the front page of
next week's *Rolling Stone*, but in Canada where everybody is, as you said
before, a little bit more humble and reserved, they just want to sweep that
under the carpet.

"The unfortunate part is that it was a guy who had some problems and people mistook it as one of those sort of rock 'n roll rebel stories, which it totally is not. And then, me, being the frontman of the band, everybody pictures me in the driver's seat. I wasn't even there, you know? I was actually sitting down with Kim Mitchell and the guys from [hip-hop group] Dream Warriors, ready to have my first beverage of the evening [laughs]. That's how that turned out."

Daryl Gray, like many musicians, took the changes in stride and found positives in the change as well, a chance to perform for a more intimate audience.

"I think we all missed playing the big sheds but none of us could say that we hadn't missed playing the bars either, because I think that any musician will tell you that playing in a packed bar can be way more fun than playing in a packed arena. It's just a perception difference, like in the packed bar everybody is so close that you can see the sweat dripping off the ends of their noses."

Derry Grehan: "It's tough, because you have this immense popularity and then it starts to wane, as it does with everybody, and man, it's a short ride. It's like going to Six Flags Park and you get on this amazing roller coaster ride, but it's over too fast and you just want it to last forever, but it doesn't."

I can't really say that the nineties were all awful for me. In that decade I ultimately did get to have my first experiences with recording with signed acts and established artists and touring. But I wasn't me. I would lie in interviews, and when the hipster weekly art rags would interview one of my bands, I would make fun of the very people who influenced me. I cut my hair, wore the ridiculous fucking polyester shirts that every dumb-ass modern rock band of the mid- to late-nineties wore (we all looked like bad rock versions of the cast of *Swingers*). I had to fight my every instinct as a player just to land gigs. In the end, this probably forced me into being versatile, which has served me well as musician over the years. But I wasn't happy. I wasn't me. I fell into the trap that so many artists fall into, chasing trends, chasing new acts to play with that didn't really move me. The dream started to work against me, and I started to forget why I got into music in the first place.

But here's the thing ... at the end of the day, no matter what the situation, the truth comes out. You have to face what you are and who you are. Every musician in this world has a genetic imprint that becomes apparent when they sing or play their instrument. When that is coupled with the real inspirations of their youth, magic can happen. Otherwise you're just faking it.

Fortunately for me, and the fans and artists of the heavy metal genre, burgeoning technological advances (while admittedly killing big parts of the recording industry and the highway to rock 'n roll as we knew it) brought those factions driven underground together in a way that breathed new life into the music that rocked us so hard in the eighties and early nineties.

HARD ROCK OF AGES: STANDING THE TEST OF TIME

both love and hate the Internet. I love it as a communication tool, but I hate the word. I guess this is just part of my ancient way of viewing the world, but it really bothers me that so much of the way we reach out these days is intangible. In a world of MP3s, emails, and Facebook, I'm a straight-up vinyl, phone calls, and (real) face time-loving Luddite. The word *Internet* just sucks me out of my stylized comfort zone, kinda like looking at an album cover on an iPad when you really want to feel the cardboard jacket under your fingertips. When I think about most of the messed-up shit or disagreements that I have been involved with in the last decade, it usually started with a bunch of Internet cyber ga-ga ... problems that just don't seem to happen when you communicate eyeball-to-eyeball. We all know how illegal downloading has drastically altered the face of the music industry, and a lot of great music people (good friends of mine, in fact) have been seriously hurt by the changes over the last twelve years or so. Certainly, the traditional way for an artist to make dreams come true has changed in turn.

And yet, the fact of the matter is that the Internet has saved my favourite type of music. That's right, the Internet SAVED HEAVY METAL!

Okay, that statement could be construed as overly dramatic, and really, the statement could be applied to any type of music that has fallen out of favour. The Internet really lays out a musical smorgasbord that is open for everyone to sample from a wide variety of fare (and steal it easily), and really, this has made the modern listener immune to the consultation of marketing pressure and contrived trends from the big record labels (at least for the most part ... God love 'em, they are still trying). Now the pressure and contrivance comes from the people themselves, man, the new gatekeepers we call bloggers, the self-appointed experts of the best way to spend your time surfing. Anyone passionate enough about a subject can reach out and grab ya via our wonderful wireless world of connectivity.

Through my musically shame-ridden late nineties, as I'd come home from a particularly uninspiring rehearsal or gig (okay, they weren't *all* bad, I played with some great musicians), I would comfort myself by holing up in the secrecy of my apartment and trolling for info on my favourite bands of yesteryear. It was like a warm blanket, a comfort to go digging and find old magazine ads, promo shots, and articles from back in the day. Many of the sites I would go to were fan-based, and there were forums where people posted their memories, thoughts, and opinions, as well as links to other materials. I started to realize that there were communities forming, and that I really wasn't alone in my desire for the sounds and looks of the eighties-inspired bands. I was also amazed at how many never gave up and were still forging musical pathways that the mainstream music press was not alerting the public to.

The Internet's provision of mutually beneficial access has also been a major part of the revitalization of this music. Just as it has allowed bands to find and target the demographics that may have once seemed lost to them, it has also allowed the fans to reach out and express what the music has meant to them over the years.

Says Gerry McGhee, "The Internet is an amazing thing. I remember there was a video up (on YouTube) for 'Still the One' and it was used with all these pictures behind [a lyric video]. One of the lyrics was wrong so I emailed and said 'Hey, by the way that lyric's wrong' and the person who put it up came back and said 'I can't believe it's you, I'll fix it right away!' After a little chatting back and forth I asked where she was, and she said Mexico City. You know, we never played there, and when you see [old videos on YouTube] it's like that's why all that kind of stuff still sells today out of here, because it's opened up [by the Internet]. We didn't really care if the Canadian music industry recognized us as long as the people did, and when somebody says 'Hey man, I remember driving around town listening to *Young, Wild and Free* in my '72 Monte Carlo, cranking it up,' that's the people who I'm impressed with."

This "by the people, for the people"-fuelled resurgence in the popularity of metal and hard rock does beg a question in this closing chapter. After all those early years vying for the attention of the record labels, did the bands feel that they ever truly established any sort of legacy or respect from the Canadian music industry machine?

Don Wolf, who went on to re-form and secure White Wolf a new record deal and a European tour in the mid-2000s while also continuing his musical journey through vocal coaching, writing, and producing for other artists, had this to say about the industry's perceptions of White Wolf's contributions to the Canadian music landscape.

"Not sure if it was really given the chance here in Canada, and we seemed to have a bigger following in the U.S. than in Canada … I think we were part of the beginnings of a metal revolution in Canada with bands like Kick Axe, Helix, and other bands of those days, but were never really recognized here for that — oh well!"

Russ Dwarf says, "I don't think so, really. I think we've always been the underdogs. We get overlooked a lot, but c'est la vie. The industry is one thing, but the people that actually listen to the songs, that's the real thing. And I don't know, it's always been our lot in life in Canada for some reason, but I don't let it upset me. I'm a total patriot, I love Canada and I'm a Canadian through and through."

With a gig singing with Canadian legends Moxy, a new acoustic album in the can, and a new Russ Dwarf electric album to be produced by legendary producer Andy Johns forthcoming, Russ is still very active in music. His Killer Dwarfs comrade Darrell Millar is also forging a new path to success with his band Automan, where he moves out from behind the kit to be the frontman.

"We had a Juno nomination, video awards, and a gold record. I mean, it reflected what we did," says Sven Gali's Andy Frank. "The more interesting part for me is that we played a couple of gigs in the last few years. Everyone is old and shitty and all that, but on the other hand the thing is to remember the fun times and the gigs in 1990, '91, '92. It really was a part of that time for people who were of the right age in Canada. It was way cooler to me to know that we were in this thing, and as a band we were very close to our audience. We lived with them, we partied with them every day, so we actually have a lot of friends from that time. To know twenty-five years later that the songs and gigs that you played are really good, positive memories for a lot of people in Canada is way cooler to me, to know that you've made a tiny little impact creatively on people in the early nineties."

"I will tell you the first answer that came to my mind," says Carl Dixon. "My answer is no, but I feel like we're a part of the Canadian rock audience's history. Coney Hatch has not been measured, quantified, awarded, or nominated for a single award in the Canadian industry where the money guys are. But where the listeners are, we have been recognized."

Having had the pleasure of working with Carl in both full band formats and as an acoustic duo, I can say with absolute certainty that this is a man who thrives off the pure energy of human interaction. Dixon's post-Coney Hatch years saw him playing numerous roles as a professional musician. He had notable stints as a guitarist/keyboardist with Canadian legend April Wine prior to landing a prestigious gig as the lead vocalist for The Guess Who, filling the role left vacant by one of Canada's greatest musical exports, Burton Cummings. It was during his stint with The Guess Who that I first met Carl. A booking agent by the name of Ken Sherwood had witnessed my band Crash Kelly playing somewhere, and he thought we would be a good fit for a support slot on a Carl Dixon solo gig. At that point, which would have been mid-2000s, I would have been afraid to look like a geek by gushing to Carl how much I loved Coney Hatch, but naturally I was eager to make an impression on someone I admired. Fortunately, we made a good impression on Carl's daughter Carlin, and there was talk of Carl and I doing some work together ... this was thrilling stuff.

On April 14, 2008, Carl was involved in a serious automobile accident in Australia while working with his daughter Lauren on a TV show called *The Saddle Club*. Carl was in an induced coma for days as his body healed from the severe trauma. He was told that it was his healthy lifestyle and peak physical condition that saw him survive the crash. Of course, there is a lot more to that story, but it is one that Carl will tell in his own book, in his own words.

I will say that the first time I saw him after the accident was two years later. I had just returned from a South American tour with Nelly Furtado and received an email asking me if I'd like to play guitar with Carl and an all-star band featuring Mark Santers on drums and Tim Harrington (Aldo Nova, Honeymoon Suite) on bass. We would be performing a night of Coney Hatch music, so naturally I jumped at the chance. When Carl came to my house to run over guitar parts I could see that he was still dealing with the physical challenges of his accident. I was completely in awe of how great the guy looked compared to when I had seen pictures of him at the Full Metal Package benefit concert that featured Helix, Brighton Rock, Russ Dwarf, and Andy Curran's Soho 69. His attitude in light of all that had happened to him was astounding, but I could tell that this was someone who had been through the wringer.

But man, when it came to gig time, I saw a transformation that continues to inspire me to this day. The music that was coming from inside this man was also outwardly altering him, healing him ... at one point he was on top of the PA, delivering the goods in a glory that was very much in the present. What I saw that night was nothing less than the physical manifestation of a vocation, a life's calling. I was honoured to be a part of it. A re-formed Coney Hatch recently signed a recording contract with Frontiers Records, home to Def Leppard, Whitesnake, and a host of other melodic hard rock heavyweights, and the band is lined up for a number of major festival appearances in the summer of 2013.

Brian Vollmer realized that building his brand back up from zero was going to be a slow process. (One year the sole Helix gig was an outdoor concert at a Ski-Doo festival in June, on the grass, to a handful of people). So he focused in on small, manageable goals and kept his eye on the bottom line.

"I basically realized that it all begins with the dollar and making money, so I picked my hometown and I got a gig there and I just made sure that we filled the seats and the guy that was hiring us made money. I just slowly did that and I ended up going back with Bernie Aubin [owner of the Canadian

Classic Rock booking agency and drummer to this day for The Headpins] for western Canadian dates and I just slowly built the band back up."

And how did the Internet help Brian bring Helix back from the grave that grunge dug?

"When I took over the band in the mid-nineties, one of the first things I did was I went to an old high school chum, Ron Kingyens, who had worked at [electronics retailer] Radio Shack as long as I'd been in Helix, so he knew computers inside out and he actually had approached me previously about doing the website. So I handed things over to him, just sent him all the info and he put together an award-winning website. Part of the website was the merchandise store and part of the money I make is from that. We communicate probably more with our fans now on Facebook, because Facebook is immediate, whereas the website basically I update once a week. You can find the dates and things like that, but for immediate news on the band we use Facebook."

One of the things that makes Brian's website so compelling is the vast and very open history that he lays out — the story of Helix as told via *www.planethelix.com* is a compelling story of success, failure, redemption, and all points in between. It was through Helix's website that I reached out to Brian over the years, planting the seed that should he ever need a guitar player, I was up for the gig ... it only took four years of trying (and a referral from my journalist friend Mitch Lafon!) to actually get an audition with Helix. It was for the bassist position, and the feeling of walking out of Brian's elaborately designed, MTV *Cribs*-featured house (a result of Brian's and his amazing wife Lynda's incredible imagination and a lot of sweat equity) as a newly minted member of Helix has stayed with me long after.

It's funny to think that after all those years of taking millions of dollars of record company money to create a larger-than-life image, it is the DIY aesthetic and grassroots honesty that have helped resurrect the Helix brand. Of course, this was also aided by Brian's commitment to doing the absolute best he could with the resources he has had at his disposal.

"I learned very good business principles from Bill [Seip, manager] when he was with us. As soon as we do a gig I am usually doing a breakdown sheet the next day. Always take care of your books and know where your money is going. I'm pretty tight with cash. I'm always looking for the cheapest way to do things without sacrificing quality. Other aspects of the music business have changed, but keeping track of that stuff hasn't."

Having worked with Brian on three Helix records in the last four years, I can attest to the veracity of this statement. I have been a proud business partner on three Helix records that were independently financed by Brian (my time as a co-producer, session musician, and project co-ordinator were counted as an investment), and these recordings have been the first of my career of which I have received regular royalty cheques for actual record sales, a source of great pride to both Brian and myself. It has also been amazing to have developed a songwriting relationship with him. A few songs have even seen us enjoy some chart action on rock radio. To hear a song that I had a hand in writing coming out of my car radio speakers, performed by the first band I ever heard in concert, is the stuff of that rock 'n roll fantasy that Bad Company was talking about.

It has also been amazing to watch as bands like Helix, Honeymoon Suite, Brighton Rock, Coney Hatch, and almost all of the others mentioned in this book have come roaring back on the festival circuits, many of them with new record deals from any number of labels (big and small) that realize that while record sales are still in dramatic decline, the people that *are* buying records are the ones who grew up with the love of the tangible product, the fans of the classic rock artists, in particular hard rock and heavy metal artists. Canadian metal is well represented at major melodic rock festivals in Europe like Firefest in England, the M3 and Rocklahoma festivals in the U.S., open air festivals like Wacken in Germany, and Sweden Rock in, uh … Sweden. It is interesting to note that fans of heavier metal seem to be impervious to trends and change. A more loyal following is seemingly passed on from generation to generation.

Mike Campagnolo says, "Razor has always had some underlying respect given to them by people who understand the metal scene, for sure. Only lately have I noticed a lot more recognition from the industry towards the band and its history. My kids can look me up on YouTube now and they usually get a kick out of that. I think the multimedia age has definitely helped with the sustainability of Razor."

"For the past ten years we have enjoyed a resurgence of popularity, but the nineties were a bit harder, mainly the early nineties, of course," says Michel Langevin. "It happened really quick as well. In 1990, we were touring with Faith No More, Soundgarden, Rush, and we were selling tons of albums, and then the year after, when 'Smells Like Teen Spirit' came out, it was a bit harder already for everybody playing metal. But then again, it didn't have such a negative impact on me because what are you gonna do? I'm sure everybody felt like that when The Beatles showed up, like, how can you compete with that? It's fresh air, a new decade, new crowd and all that. But it had an effect on the band and we split up for the first time in '91. That was a time in the early nineties when metal took on a bit of a low profile, but then again, soon after we were able to go to Europe and play crazy festivals because it was always healthy over there. Also, Pantera, Machine Head, Fear Factory became huge and they were flying the metal flag really high, so it came back in the picture.

"What really brings me back to Voivod is travelling, touring around the globe. We have a very loyal following and we meet our friends. Every time we go out, people show up and it's really like there were many times in Voivod's career when the band either didn't exist or it was just Piggy [guitarist] and me, or Snake [vocalist] and me, and every time we spent a couple of years on hiatuses, we would get antsy, phone each other, and find a new way of getting back on the road. When we re-formed in 2008, we started going to places we had never been before — South America, Asia, and last October we played in Russia, in Moscow, for the first time and people were chanting 'Voivod' like twenty minutes before we showed up onstage. It was truly amazing and it's really what brings me back to music. People have to understand that we have very good cult status in many places on earth, so it's easier for Voivod to re-form once in a while and go to Russia or Spain than it is for many other bands that were around in the eighties. We can always do it and people will show up. That's an advantage, some kind of a cult status, I guess."

Rob Urbinati of Sacrifice's views of how he feels the industry views heavier bands is a decidedly harsher one, no doubt an opinion forged after years of indifference even during thrash's heyday. He feels the indifference affects any band outside of a perceived Canadian mainstream sound.

"The Canadian music industry is a joke. It barely even recognizes metal, never mind Sacrifice. Bands like Blue Rodeo and Tragically Hip seem to get all the media attention when there are many people making music outside the mainstream that could actually break out internationally with a bit of a push. Mainstream Canadian rock for the most part will not do that. Even the good Canadian rock like Danko Jones is criminally overlooked in this country. Propagandhi barely gets a mention anywhere, and they are outstanding. Sacrifice had never even appeared once in a Toronto newspaper until 2009. At the end of it all, we don't need recognition from Blue Rodeo or Red Rider fans, but it does piss me off that bands I like are overlooked on their own soil."

I think we've established that being a Canadian rock star rarely means sustained financial security, even at the peak of a band's popularity. Bills need to paid, and of course that means taking on other forms of employment, inside or outside the music industry. One of the most fascinating examples of an intermingling of two seemingly disparate worlds is Killer Dwarfs guitarist Mike Hall's decision to enlist in the Canadian Armed Forces as a guitar-playing soldier.

"In an effort to have a more contemporary sound and approach, the CF began recruiting guitarists a few years back. I always saw the U.S. bands advertising for musicians but never the Canadians. I jumped at the chance. I was tired of hustling, and I was the second man hired in 2009. There was an audition process — send in a tape and bio. If they liked what they heard, they would fly you out for a live audition. Because of my experience, education, versatility, and ability I was granted a 6A qualification. This means there is actually no musical training necessary.

"They offered me the job. I was ready to go and join one of the six bands in the Canadian Forces. But first ... boot camp. The thing is, I am a soldier first, and I'm good with that. Some musicians might not be. I took all the same military training as any other new recruit. It was tough at forty-seven years of age, but I showed up in shape, bought into the program 100 percent, and left four months later a beast of a man. Because of my 6A qualification, I was promoted to corporal upon graduation from BMQ [basic military qualification]. I hadn't touched a guitar the whole time.

"The Music Branch sent me out to Winnipeg, where they were in the process of creating a big RCAF Show band. This band has some of the best players and vocalists in the CF. We do everything you could imagine, the latest pop hits, new country, classic rock, metal, disco, etc. I have travelled all over the world with this band. We perform for the troops, represent Canada at military tattoos [military music festivals], play various government functions, community events, fundraisers, cocktail parties, and concerts at the Canadian embassy in Washington, D.C. It's fun. Lots of travel ... it's a dream come true for me. I'm never bored and practise every chance I have.

"In 2011, I was sent to PLQ [Primary Leadership Qualification] for two months of senior NCO [non-commissioned officer] training. A few months after that I was promoted to sergeant, which is the rank I hold today. This is a senior NCO rank. No other trade would move people up this fast.

"I went over to Afghanistan in March 2011 and performed for the troops in Kandahar with my old buddies in [Toronto band] the Carpet Frogs. Because I am a full-time soldier, I had to be armed and ready to go if something went wrong. I had some extra training over and above my 'musician' trade before I went. Thankfully, I didn't need to use it. Nick Sinopoli [lead singer for the Carpet Frogs] was laughing when I walked out of my room in my desert combat uniform with a 9mm Browning strapped to my leg!

"In the spring of 2012 a bunch of us appeared on a national TV show, a reality show called *Canada Sings*. We kicked ass and won $25,000, which we donated to the Soldier On program, an organization that helps CF members and their families cope with injury and various unique aspects of life in the military."

Another musician who tried another career path was Slik Toxik's Nick Walsh, but not before exploring a different musical life in the mid-nineties.

"After the Slik thing, I had written a batch of songs and put together another band which was very short-lived, called Raised on Mars. That project found me sort of casting myself within that alternative rock movement that was going on at the time, and I don't want to say grunge, but I would say more like things that were alternative like Smashing Pumpkins, different tones, you know? I was getting into different bands at the time, and in every scene good and bad comes out of it.

"So I was into what I felt were some of the good bands and they were starting to influence me, and they also cleaned all the garbage that was within our sort of [metal] genre. After that didn't happen for me, I thought, *You know, I'm gonna try something completely different.* I've been a character most of my life and people have told me I should get into acting. So I tried my hand at it. I did some bit parts on some shows and some movies and some commercial work and so forth, but you know, come the early 2000s, I had opened a recording studio and when I started recording with other bands and seeing the fire that was still within me because of the passion of other people, I decided *I'm going to just start doing this. I own my own studio, and I don't care if it takes me one year or five years or ten years to write my story again, but this is who I am, this is what I do.* It took a while to come back into my own, and once I did then I realized … I am what I am, just like Popeye said. And you might as well embrace that to the max; don't try to cater to anybody else, and eventually your time will come around, because the bottom line to me is these people that I call leap-froggers, the people that jump from bandwagon to bandwagon or whatever, they never succeed because they are never honest with what they do.

"I think more than pop culture dictates trends and so forth — I think honesty rules at the end of the day and people can smell crap from a mile away. When you are just yourself, whether it's good, bad, or subjective to anybody's opinion, it usually prevails. I mean, there are so many artists out there, especially Canadian artists, songwriters, Neil Young, all these guys, that people would look at and they'd go like, 'This guy can't sing … but man, he writes a hell of a song and you know it's him.' So at the end of the day that's why they find success, because they're honest with themselves and they're honest with everybody else. That's what I think people within our genre have done. Even some of the people from back in the eighties that I listen to, they're now playing at these Monsters of Rock boat cruises and the M3 Rock Festival, Rocklahoma, and all this stuff. There's a place for everybody and there's obviously a market for everybody, too."

Aside from his acting work, Walsh has since gone on to front two relatively successful projects, Revolver and Famous Underground. I was proud to be able to work with Nick in Revolver as a co-guitarist alongside Gene Scarpelli, son of Goddo's Gino Scarpelli. Nick and I bonded quickly over a shared love of the same types of music, but also over our struggles to rediscover our musical identities. It has been gratifying for me to see Nick stick to his musical guns while also being open to current influences. Famous Underground's recent signing to a European management and record deal is testament to Nick's hard work and vision.

Harry Hess from Harem Scarem has had much success in his post-Harem Scarem life (the band actually reconvened in 2013 for a re-record of their classic *Mood Swings* album and live festival appearances), but he is still searching for what really defines success.

"I'm signed to Universal Music Publishing as a writer. I have travelled the world the last three years writing with Universal writers all around the world, people in Sweden that have written number one Billboard pop tracks. I went to Nashville and wrote with guys that have written number one hits for Rascal Flatts, Tim McGraw, all that stuff, and oddly enough, the vibe when we're having lunch or at the end of the session is that they don't know [what defines success] either, you know? [laughs]. They'll look at me and say, 'I haven't had a hit in five years, I'm not really sure what I'm going to do,' and I'm like, 'What?' I've worked with guys that have worked with Madonna and Kylie Minogue and Jessica Simpson and one of the guys who I'm good friends with said, 'Yeah, I've got nothing going on right now and I don't really know what I'm going to do next week.'

"If you let that dictate whether you're successful or not, you can look at anybody in a twenty-year career and say, 'Wow, look what this person has done and what they've accomplished. They've sold a lot of records, they've made a lot of money,' but I'll bet you at some point in that month or that week or that year they had a time when they felt they were not successful. I mean, it goes up and down, and over a long career you will not have success every year greater than the last year, so at some point it is inevitable that you'll look back and go, 'Oh, I'm not doing so well' or 'I didn't do so well that year.' The point is to keep going and try for another success, and if you're good at what you do, it will probably happen.

"I look at it completely differently now than I did when I was eighteen or nineteen, because I have the luxury of perspective to look back at it and say, 'Well this is what I considered to be success.' But if I were nineteen and sold seven million records out of the gate, I wouldn't know what to say. I mean, I was at Warner when Alanis Morissette accepted her plaque for whatever it was, like, diamond in Canada, and she was like in her early twenties at the time and she gets up there, accepts the plaque and goes, 'Well, only way to go from here. That's down.' [laughs] I thought that was fucking awesome. Somebody that's like twenty-one, twenty-two years old accepts this plaque in the middle of — you remember what that was like. I mean, it was unstoppable. But she had the presence of mind to know … and that's exactly what happened."

A very rarified group of artists goes on to make a great living solely by performing their own original music. The reality for most of the groups I've talked to is that they have had to involve themselves in a number of endeavours to sustain a living. The best term I ever heard for a mix of musical and non-musical jobs came from Helix's Brent Doerner, who, when questioned about what he did for a living, replied, "I'm a Guitarpenter." Perfect.

So if you ain't in it for the money, ya gotta be in for love, love, love. Or at least the memories of a life out of the ordinary, and the experiences that the adventure has brought to fruition.

David Rashed, Haywire: "When I look back, the thirteen years with the band were some of the best times with many experiences. We were fortunate to be able to travel and experience all that we did. The band really has a special connection, and when we regroup, we're reminded of that."

Stacey Blades, L.A. Guns: "I cherish those times of busting my ass on the scene in Toronto in the late eighties and early nineties. I think it made me stronger as a musician, seeing that there is greatness there but at the same time a big roadblock. Knocking down that roadblock, I'm kind of proud I did that."

Russ Graham, Killer Dwarfs: "It was the best thing. I lived my dreams, my life was great … it is great. I'm totally proud of the Dwarts. Great players, great writers, and troopers in the rock wars."

Derry Grehan, Honeymoon Suite: "When we go out on tour there are a lot of older fans now who are in their forties and fifties, and it's really nice when they say 'I met my wife at your show, and the music is a memory for me.' The music brings back a great memory of a time when they were younger."

When you hear the word *memories*, it is so easily to immediately associate that with nostalgia. And let's face it, nostalgia plays a huge part in any sort of resurgence of music from a past era. I know that when I put on a Slik Toxik record, a Helix record, or a Coney Hatch record, I am immediately transported back to a time of innocence, a time before I knew things I wish I still didn't know about the world. It feels warm and safe, which is why these bands and their fans find each other: to celebrate those times. But to say that the value of this music in the current day begins and ends there does a disservice to the work these artists put in. It also does a disservice to Canadian history, because the impact that these acts have had on the culture *is* relevant, and it *is* important. And yet, in any book about Canadian music I have ever read, these heavy metal and hard rock heroes have been relegated to footnote status at best. For someone like me, who has been blessed to make a life of music because of the influence and impact of these artists, this is simply unacceptable. In my youth, their music provided me with shelter from the cold world outside, inspiration to achieve, and ultimately a vehicle which has allowed me to travel the world. In my current gig with Nelly Furtado, I have had the opportunity to play on big stages with massive production, just like the ones I would scribble on my binders in school. I am indebted to Nelly, a world-class musician and beautiful human being, for allowing me to fully savour those moments in my leather jacket and motorcycle boots, with a low-slung Les Paul or Kramer 84 on my shoulder. Her generosity in allowing me to be that twelve-year-old living out his dream is something I will forever be grateful for.

This is a book about the pursuit of the rock 'n roll dream in Canada, through the eyes of artists that inspired me to go for the same dream, or at least my interpretation of it. And with the focus of this music book being Canadian artists, I had to ask the question: Do you feel your nationality helps define you as an artist?

Brian Vollmer, Helix: "I find that people are people. I find there is good and bad and it doesn't matter if you're an American band or a Canadian band. There are British guys that are great, there's British guys that are assholes. There are Canadian guys that are great, and there are Canadian guys who are assholes."

Darby Mills, Headpins: "My nationality defines me as a human ... O Canada! I am truly graced and thankful for anyone that has found a smile, a hope, or even a tear in the music I have helped to create. My wish is to do so for as long as people continue to listen ... or maybe even after that! [laughs]"

Derry Grehan, Honeymoon Suite: "I'm proud to be a Canadian, and I think we have a real Canadian identity and a good history with people."

Rick Hughes, Sword/Saints & Sinners: "One thing is for sure: I am a French Canadian who loves to sing in English."

Lee Aaron: "Yes, especially as a rock artist overseas. They love Canadian rock bands there and feel we have a unique Canadian sound. I wear that badge proudly."

So yeah ... there is a whole full circle thing going on here with this rock 'n roll story. This story began with hockey, and it seems only fitting to end it with hockey. Is there a correlation between Canada's national sport and some of the nation's hard rock and heavy metal heroes?

Brian Vollmer, Helix: "Well, the biggest comparison I'll use to a hockey team is that when you walk onstage every night you want to do a good job, but there are some nights you just can't find the groove, and I would imagine hockey teams are the same ... they always walk on the ice to win but sometimes they can't find the groove!"

Russ Graham, Killer Dwarfs: "I come from a huge sports family and I played hockey of course, I'm Canadian — hockey and beer. I think when you play those arenas it's like a dream come true because you've gone down and seen Rush every New Year's Eve at Maple Leaf Gardens."

Gerry McGhee, Brighton Rock: "We actually had a Brighton Rock hockey team that me and Steve Skreebs [bassist] played on for many years. We were also on a rock 'n roll all-star team with Andy Curran, Carl Dixon, Larry Gowan, Rik Emmett [Triumph], and a whole bunch of guys."

Sean Kilbride, Haywire: "Absolutely. When I was a kid, the first concerts I went to were at the Halifax Forum, home of the Nova Scotia Voyageurs of the AHL. When KISS, April Wine, or Cheap Trick would come to town, that's where they'd play. When Haywire first broke, there was a gig in Dominion, Cape Breton, at the local arena on a sweltering summer day, and I remember us walking around the back of the boards from the stage and watching through the Plexiglas as the crowd got hosed down by firemen. Whether it was a rink in Deep River, Ontario, or the Calgary Saddledome, there was usually the smell of hockey. We opened for Corey

Hart at the old Montreal Forum and they put us in the visitors' dressing room. I thought I had truly arrived."

Nick Walsh, Slik Toxik: "Definitely! Being a Canadian kid seeing concerts at hockey arenas made playing those arenas a true dream to aspire to. And as odd as this sounds, team-wise, I found a band to have the same sort of positions: Centre: Lead Vocals, Wingers: Guitars, Defence: Bass, and Goalie: Drums! [laughs]"

Carl Dixon, Coney Hatch: "Oh, the goalie is the drummer [laughs]. And yeah, I often felt like when we were on stage the singer is the centre, the playmaker, and right and left wing were the bass player and guitar player. It sounds like the French Connection storyline for Coney Hatch, where everybody was hitting their part just right and we all anticipated one another's moves and successfully completed the plays. That's what a band feels like onstage when the energy is right and everybody is on and you're responding to the energy of the crowd. It's very similar to hockey. The one thing I found, because I got to meet a lot of pro hockey players over the years, was that all the hockey players I knew secretly wanted to be musicians. And all the musicians I knew, from Canada at least, wanted to be hockey players."

In some small way, my hope in writing this book is for people to see Canadian heavy metal in a similar light to the way we view hockey ... as a source of great national pride, a part of our cultural history. I'll spare you the analogies about well-placed hits, blood, sweat, and tears, and coming up through the minor league ranks for a crack at the big time ... but allow me one indulgence.

My dad, Des Kelly, was a right winger with the Memorial Cup–winning Barrie Flyers of the OHL, and he also spent time with the notorious Johnstown Jets of the EHL in the fifties (the team that the movie *Slapshot* was modelled after). He played in Johnstown alongside his brother Orville "Crash" Kelly, whose nickname I borrowed for my glam rock band. One thing he always told me when he coached me in my modest minor hockey days was, "You never score on the shot you don't take." All the bands in this book had the balls to take their shot in one of the toughest, yet greatest music markets in the world. And at some point, in some way, each one of them managed to put the puck in the back of the net.

AFTERWORD

Y ou know, I bitch and moan a lot about how the mid-nineties were such a huge drag ... and in a lot of ways they were for me. But really, it was the era in which I truly cut my professional teeth. And I did enjoy a lot of things about my time playing with different bands of different genres. I was forced to be a diverse musician, as my first musical true love had fallen hopelessly and painfully out of style. I recognize now that this is in no way a bad thing. Being a true musician is not necessarily about simply absorbing and reflecting one set of influences (as totally awesome as those influences may be!). It is about taking the passion of our early musical loves and allowing them to mix and merge with the inevitable exposure we receive to the wide world of opportunity that exists within different genres. We don't *need* to deny our roots, but sometimes we need to accept that we need to be flexible and open to circumstances (musical or otherwise) that we do not and cannot control.

For me, the way I survived, and hell, even sometimes thrived, as a player in the nineties and the first decade of the millennium was by allowing the heavy metal and hard rock that is in my genetic makeup to inform the other styles of music I was playing. When my good friend Thom McKercher, the director of Classics and Jazz at Universal Music Canada introduced me in 2006 to Charles "Chuck" Daellenbach of the Canadian Brass and the owner of Opening Day Entertainment Group, I was presented with a unique opportunity: to make classical guitar recordings, not as a *classical* guitarist, but as a rock player who had studied the classics. It was amazing appearing on classical radio stations and doing promo tours of high-end bookstores and explaining the connection between composers like Tarrega, Albeniz, and Villa Lobos, and heavy metal guitar. As my A&R man Thom put in a print ad for *The #1 Classical Guitar Album* (the title refers to the popular repertoire, not the player in this case!), "Not all great riffs are played at 100db"! I'm pretty sure that was the first classical guitar album ad to ever run in *Brave Words & Bloody Knuckles* magazine, by the way.

I am also very lucky to get called upon to do sessions with some of Canada's best producers, and I feel good knowing that it is *because* of my influences and the way I play that I am called, not in spite of those things. My good pal, amazing guitarist, and formative influence, Tim Welch of Sylum/National Velvet/Images in Vogue and many others always reminds me of something when I'm playing him music I've been working on. Even when I *think* I'm sounding like someone else when I'm working on a project, even when I'm *trying* to sound like someone else ... I'm always going to end up sounding like me. And that me is not made up of the latest hipster sounds. My musical fingerprint is the manifestation of a love for a music I discovered in a hockey dressing room, that inspired me on a hockey arena stage, and that has ultimately led to me tread the boards of venues that I never thought (but always dreamed) I'd get to perform in.

I am by no means a rock star. But I am a rock fan, and this fanaticism has gifted me with the experiences I currently get to enjoy. I am so very grateful to have played "Devil's Deck" with Carl Dixon, "Helluvatime" with Nick Walsh, and to play "Rock You" as a member of Helix. I am also grateful that the lessons these artists have taught me allow me to make a living as a musician. It is not lost on me that it is through their sacrifices that I get to be a small part of this glorious lineage, this

Canadian heavy metal and hard rock history that I am hoping *Metal on Ice* will help bring into the light. Preferably a spotlight, on an 80-foot arena rock stage with rows of Marshall stacks, a double bass drum kit on a sky-high riser, and enough pyro to rival the Northern Lights.

Rock You.

SELECTED DISCOGRAPHY
(The Platters that Mattered to a Young Sean Kelly)

This discography does not constitute a complete list of bands or their recordings ... this is, very selfishly, I might add, a collection of the recordings that resonated with me in my youth, and continue to do so to this day. Or to put it another way: If I invited you over to my basement studio for a beer, I might spin some of these as a means of introducing you to my favourite Canadian hard rock and metal bands.

HELIX

No Rest for the Wicked (1983 Capitol/EMI)
Walkin' The Razor's Edge (1984 Capitol/EMI)
Long Way to Heaven (1985 Capitol/EMI)
Wild in the Streets (1987 Capitol/EMI)
Back for Another Taste (1990 Capitol/EMI)

CONEY HATCH

Coney Hatch (1982 Anthem/Mercury)
Outta Hand (1983 Anthem/Mercury)
Friction (1985 Anthem/Mercury)

KICK AXE

Vices (1984 Pasha/CBS)
Welcome to the Club (1985 Pasha/CBS)

WHITE WOLF

Standing Alone (1984 RCA)
Endangered Species (1985 RCA)

ANVIL

Metal on Metal (1982 Attic)
Forged in Fire (1983 Attic)
Strength of Steel (1987 Metal Blade)

KILLER DWARFS

Stand Tall (1986 Maze/A&M)
Big Deal (1988 Epic)
Dirty Weapons (1990 Epic)
Method to the Madness (1992 Epic)

BIG HOUSE

Big House (1991 BMG)

HAREM SCAREM

Harem Scarem (1991 WEA)
Mood Swings (1993 WEA)

SLIK TOXIK

Smooth n' Deadly EP (1991 Capitol/EMI)
Doin' the Nasty (1991 Capitol/EMI)

SVEN GALI

Sven Gali (1992 BMG)

BRIGHTON ROCK

Young Wild and Free (1986 WEA)
Take a Deep Breath (1988 WEA)
Love Machine (1991 WEA)

SURE

It Ain't Pretty Being Easy (1990 A&M)

HONEYMOON SUITE

Honeymoon Suite (1984 WEA)
The Big Prize (1985 WEA)
Racing After Midnight (1988 WEA)

SWORD

Metallized (1986 Aquarius)
Sweet Dreams (1988 Aquarius)

HAYWIRE

Don't Just Stand There (1987 Attic)
Nuthouse (1990 Attic)

LEE AARON

Metal Queen (1984 Attic)
Lee Aaron (1987 Attic)
Body Rock (1989 Attic)

HEADPINS

Turn it Loud (1982 Solid Gold)
Line of Fire (1983 Solid Gold)

toronto

Lookin' for Trouble (1980 Solid Gold)
Head On (1981 Solid Gold)
Get It on Credit (1982 Solid Gold)

voivod

Killing Technology (1987 Noize)
Dimension Hatröss (1988 Noize)
Nothingface (1989 Mechanic/MCA)

SACRIFICE

Forward to Termination (1987 Diabolic/Metal Blade)
Soldiers of Misfortune (1990 Fringe/Metal Blade)

RAZOR

Evil Invaders (1985 Attic)
Malicious Intent (1986 Attic)

WITH REGRETS: BANDS THAT deserved A mention

A s this book was delivered into my editor's able hands, I was still nagged by the fact that I didn't really mention a few deserving bands. They may not have played a big a role in my own early music journey, but I would later come to either interact with members of the bands or discover their importance. In some cases, I just didn't have time to give them their due properly in context of the narrative. Anyway, enough lame excuses … a doffing of the cap to:

Triumph: Rik Emmett, Gil Moore, and Mike Levine, your arena rock history is touched upon briefly in the book. *Thunder Seven*, *Sport of Kings*, and *Surveillance* all served as backdrop to my musical youth, and the amazing albums that came before these were crucial to the development of Canadian hard rock … I look forward to diving further into your history in future musings (and Phil X, your contributions via the *Edge of Excess* album are duly noted!). If it seems criminal they are not in a book about Canadian hard rock and heavy metal, well … it may be. But there is a bigger story about this consummate power trio that I think might have to be written in a book featuring another consummate power trio … I've said too much.

Goddo: I never owned a Goddo album until I began playing with guitarist Gino Scarpelli's son Gene in the bands Revolver and then Crash Kelly. I was missing out. Greg Godovitz, Doug Inglis, and Gino served up classic high-energy rock that influenced a ton of people via Polydor Records albums that were staples of the early Canadian hard rock diet. Read Greg's book *Travels With My Amp* to get the full Goddo story, and many more. Guitar players could also do worse for themselves than to go check out the guitar playing of both Scarpelli men, who are blues rockers par excellence.

Santers: Rick Santers, Mark Santers, and Rick Lazaroff were, by their own website's admission, "Underrated, and under the radar," but a listen to their back catalogue yields some fine melodic rock rewards. Each member is a stellar musician (Rick Santers was recruited by Triumph as a second guitarist/keyboardist/vocalist on their Sport of Kings tour, and also contributed compositionally to the album of the same name), and the crowd I saw them draw at a reunion show in Toronto a few years back confirms that Santers was a much-loved and important part of the hard rock story in Canada.

Moxy: Pioneers of the mid-seventies through early eighties Canadian hard rock scene, they were another band that made an impact in the U.S. via Texas DJ Joe Anthony. Led by the vocals of Buzz Shearman and the guitar of Earl Johnson, the band toured with the likes of Black Sabbath and Boston, and even recorded two albums with legendary Aerosmith producer Jack Douglas at the helm. When you have the UK music press calling you the Canadian Led Zeppelin, it speaks volumes about your ability to speak with volume!

Reckless: Steve Madden, I picked up a vinyl copy of your 1984 album *Heart of Steel* when I was on tour recently. You were there at the beginning of hair metal in Canada, when it was still an edgier beast. Kudos for following your dream and immortalizing yourself and your band on wax.

Rockhead: Vancouver's Bob Rock is most famous as the world-class producer who spun gold and platinum for Metallica, Mötley Crüe, Kingdom Come, Bon Jovi, and other hard rock and metal giants. He was also a hit maker in his own right in Canada with The Payolas and Rock and

Hyde. But I will always be grateful for the fact that he released a self-titled album in 1992 under the moniker Rockhead. I loved this album for great Mott the Hoople-meets-hair metal tracks like "Bed of Roses" and "Chelsea Rose," but I also loved it for the fact that Bob's entire modus operandi for putting the band together was born out of a yearning to go play some classic rock in a little club somewhere in England with loud Marshall amps. The fact that he took a singer from an AC/DC cover band in British Columbia (Steve Jacks) and took the kid to Europe to open for Bon Jovi and make a bigass rock production record just kinda warms my heart. Rock took some of the loot he made from sonically realizing the rock 'n roll dreams of other bands, and then invested in his own dream, and for that he truly deserves the last name he was blessed with.

Annihilator, Varga, and Exciter, when the book about Canadian thrash metal is written, I know that your stories will be writ large and in boxcar letters. I salute your virtuosity, and the fact that all three acts are still out showing the world that Canadian thrash is second to none.

I regret wholeheartedly that I am undoubtedly missing people from this list … I wish I had the time and resources to acknowledge every band, every musician who slugged it out on this path that is so rewarding, yet so challenging. Here's hoping that the *Metal on Ice* community can extend beyond these pages and serve as a landing for all of you bands, musicians, and fans to share your stories of the pursuit of our shared passion.

Acknowledgements

hank you to:

The artists and insiders who shared their stories for this book.

Erin and Des for all of their love and support

Allister Thompson for his faith in this project and for helping me rock some of those arena stages.

The staff at Dundurn Press.

Julie Gibb and Kerry Kelly for their detailed and thoughtful transcription work.

To the Coalition Music family, thank you for helping me take *Metal on Ice* beyond the page and onto the stage!

Sean Palmerston for helping me find the thrashers!

Drew Masters and Brian Vollmer for sharing your own writing in this book.

Martin Popoff, for continuously feeding my heavy metal appetite with your great books.

SEAN KELLY

Metal on Ice

TUNES FROM CANADA'S HARD
ROCK AND HEAVY METAL HEROES

Billboard-charting guitarist Sean Kelly is a native of North Bay, Ontario. He moved to Toronto in the early 1990s to study classical guitar under renowned instructor Eli Kassner at the University of Toronto. At the same time he started to seek his fame and fortune as a rock guitarist. After playing in several local bands, he formed his own band, Crash Kelly, in which he both sang and played lead guitar. The band has released three albums via Century Media, the world's largest independent heavy metal label, and toured with hard rock legend Alice Cooper.

Sean also currently tours as lead guitarist for Grammy Award–winning superstar Nelly Furtado and has performed with and written a number of songs for many multi-platinum acts, including Helix, Carole Pope, and Rough Trade, as well as former Guns N' Roses member Gilby Clarke, former Guess Who vocalist Carl Dixon, and many other notable stars.

In the last few years, he has recorded three classical guitar albums that have won great acclaim and reached the classical music bestseller charts.

The songs of *Metal on Ice* were recorded to accompany the book and feature new versions of some of the iconic songs mentioned in the book, sung by their original singers. It will be a Fall 2013 release on Coalition Music (Records)/Warner Music Canada.

ACCLAIMED FICTION FROM DUNDURN

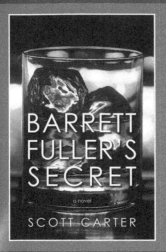

BARRETT FULLER'S
SECRET

by Scott Carter
978-1459706934
$19.99

Barrett Fuller is a world-famous and very wealthy children's author who writes under a pseudonym because he's a self-absorbed womanizer and drug-user. His life changes when he receives an extortion letter, challenging him to live up to the morals he currently espouses in his books. He is presented with a series of tasks to complete or face having his identity revealed to the public, resulting in the ruin of his financial empire.

Richard Fuller, Barrett's nephew, has a secret too, and it's one no kid should bear. He knows why his father left the family and he's never told his mother.

When the extortionist challenges Barrett to spend time with his nephew, their respective secrets move towards a collision that will change their lives forever.

Available at your favourite bookseller

DUNDURN

Visit us at

Dundurn.com | @dundurnpress | Facebook.com/dundurnpress | Pinterest.com/dundurnpress